Microfinance and Poverty Reduction

Susan Johnson and Ben Rogaly

Oxfam
(UK and Ireland)

First published by Oxfam (UK and Ireland) and ActionAid in 1997

Reprinted by Oxfam GB 1997, 1999, 2002

ISBN 0 85598 369 8

A catalogue record for this publication is available from the British Library.

Available from:

Bournemouth English Book Centre, PO Box 1496, Parkstone, Dorset, BH12 3YD, UK
tel: +44 (0)1202 712933; fax: +44 (0)1202 712930; email: oxfam@bebc.co.uk

USA: Stylus Publishing LLC, PO Box 605, Herndon, VA 20172-0605, USA
tel: +1 (0)703 661 1581; fax: +1 (0)703 661 1547; email: styluspub@aol.com

For details of local agents and representatives in other countries, consult our website:
http://www.oxfam.org.uk/publications

or contact Oxfam Publishing, 274 Banbury Road, Oxford OX2 7DZ, UK
tel: +44 (0)1865 311 311; fax: +44 (0)1865 312 600; email: publish@oxfam.org.uk

Our website contains a fully searchable database of all our titles, and facilities for secure on-line ordering.

Reprint designed, printed, and published by Oxfam GB, 274 Banbury Road, Oxford OX2 7DZ, UK.

Oxfam GB is a registered charity, no. 202 918, and is a member of Oxfam International.

Contents

Acknowledgements

The authors wish to acknowledge the major inputs of Farah Batool (Pakistan case study), Martha Romero, Stephen Fogarty and Ofelia Guttierez (Mexico case study),Helen Derbyshire and Aggie Kent (UK case study), Ousman Cham and the staff of ACTIONAID The Gambia (The Gambia case study), Juan Serrano, Emilia Ferraro and Javier Herran (Ecuador case study). Stuart Rutherford provided a major and much appreciated contribution in the form of a background paper, *A Critical Typology of Financial Services for the Poor*, as well as making comments on the text.

Thanks are also due to the following: Shahin Yaqub, for a background paper, *Macroeconomic Conditions for Successful Financial Services for Poor People*; Alfonso Castillo, and Md. Mumtaz Tanoli for additional assistance in planning and undertaking the case studies as well as commenting on the text; David Norman, Barbara Thomas and Helen Yanacopulos for research assistance. The following read and made valuable comments on the full text: Audrey Bronstein, James Copestake, Ros David, Helen Derbyshire, Heather Grady, Dot McCall, Amitava Mukherjee, Ravi Narayanan, Chris Roche, William Smith, Ines Smyth, and Ton van Zutphen. The authors are also grateful for the help and encouragement of Kirat Randhawa, Simran Rogaly, Deborah Eade, Pat Conaty, Carlos Ling, Michael Semple, Ceci Lopez, Pauline Wilson, and Nigel Twose. Any errors or omissions remain the responsibility of the authors.

Susan Johnson and Ben Rogaly

Introduction

During the 1990s, the provision of financial services dealing with very small deposits and loans — microfinance — and particularly the provision of microcredit, have been increasingly acclaimed as effective means of poverty reduction. There is continuing and quite rapid improvement in understanding how financial services for poor people can best be provided. This book sets out to draw together some of the most important lessons learned to date, as a useful resource for those considering financial interventions as well as those already involved. However, rather than setting out a single model of 'good practice', the book recommends an overall approach. In doing this, and in order to counteract the idea that credit alone can be a panacea for eradicating poverty, it reports on continuing debates about and different approaches to the provision of financial services to poor people.

Private sector non-profit organisations (referred to in this book as non-governmental organisations — NGOs) aiming to bring about reductions in poverty have become increasingly involved in providing financial services. Of those NGOs, most have experience of savings and credit, often linked to programmes of income generation. Very small deposits and loans are referred to together as 'microfinance'. This book focuses on microfinance and only briefly discusses its relationship to other development activities. The book does not cover financial service provision during complex emergencies or natural disasters, or for particular marginal or vulnerable groups, such as pastoralists or people with AIDS/HIV.

Before going further, the term 'financial services' needs explanation. Financial services are about enabling people to amass usefully large sums of cash (Rutherford, 1996). They can be divided into two main types: first, those that build up cash reserves through forgoing income. Saving does this by making deposits out of income now and so forgoing its current use in order to draw a sum from these savings in the future. Insurance performs a similar function: it allows the client to buy access to a future lump sum. Loans work in a similar way, but in reverse: they are lump sums which are given now in return for income forgone in the future.

The second main type of financial service allows assets to be converted into and out of lump sums of cash. Mortgages and pawns are the main examples of such services. A further type of service which poor people may need, but which is rarely discussed, is cash-handling, especially to allow the transmission of cash from one place to another. This is essential for long-term migrants, for example, wishing to send cash back to their relatives.

The elements of an effective approach to microfinance

The approach to microfinance proposed here has five main points. First, that NGOs should investigate existing financial services; who uses them and to what effect. Second, that before intervening directly, NGOs should assess whether they have the specialist knowledge and skills required to provide financial services themselves. Third, in order to design services which are relevant and useful to poor people, NGOs should understand local social and economic structures, and also macro-level trends. Fourth, NGOs should consider how the provision of services can be sustained in the long term. Lastly, the impact on poverty reduction should be continually assessed rather than taken for granted, which tends to happen if a microfinance intervention is covering its costs and has many low-income users.

The structure of this book

The book begins by setting out the main debates surrounding interventions to provide financial services, to provide a background to the rest of the book. Much of the discussion in this initial chapter is based on Rogaly (1996a).

In any situation there is likely to be an array of informal financial services which people are making use of. An overview of these is given in Chapter 2. There is now much greater understanding of the characteristics of such services and how they operate. The first task for an NGO proposing to intervene is to find out which services are already available to people and which additional ones they would find most useful. To do this the NGO must understand for whom, under what circumstances, and to what degree these services support or undermine livelihood strategies. This background information allows the design of financial services to be connected to an analysis of poverty and well-being, and at the same time establishes which existing services poor people may wish to retain, and which should therefore not be undermined by any new intervention. This chapter draws heavily on a background paper commissioned for the book: *A Critical Typology of Financial Services for the Poor*, by Stuart Rutherford, November 1996.

The next step suggested for an NGO is to critically and honestly assess whether it is best placed to become a provider of financial services. In the past NGOs have not always achieved success in this area, and have failed to appreciate that specific skills are required. Alternative approaches which enable the NGO to utilise its skills in mobilising, training, and working with poor people to promote rather than to provide services should be seriously considered. Another possible role for NGOs is in advocacy with governments, to persuade them to make the necessary legislative changes, and with national banking systems to encourage bankers to work with poor people.

Recent microfinance interventions have made use of a range of design features, which are discussed in Chapter 3. They have focused on reaching the poor by keeping loan sizes small, targeting women, adopting group-based lending systems, and mobilising small and frequent savings deposits, and have tended to set interest rates at higher levels than in the past. Such interventions have demonstrated that poor people can and do repay loans, that they have the ability to save, and that they can pay higher interest rates. The discussion in Chapter 3 explores the assumptions behind these design elements of microfinance schemes, and the ways that they operate in practice. It emphasises the fact that different combinations of design features suit particular macro-economic, socio-economic, and political circumstances. This suggests that interveners must continuously and critically assess the effects that elements of the design of their programme are having in practice. To do this, it is advisable to start slowly in order that growing understanding of people's uses for microfinance can lead to adaptations in design.

The fourth element of the approach set out in this book is a focus on sustainability, and this is discussed in Chapter 4. Microfinance initiatives have increasingly reported high repayment rates and the ability to cover part of the costs of providing the service. This has raised the possibility that organisations providing these services may be able to become self-sustaining, and so ensure the long-term provision of financial services to their users. NGOs involved in (or seeking to start) the provision of financial services need to take the issue of financial sustainability seriously, and ways of measuring financial self-sustainability are discussed in the chapter. However, financial sustainability is only one necessary condition for NGOs to be able to continue to provide services in the long term. The organisational structure, management, and staffing of the NGO are equally vital components. In discussing the forms of organisation that might be sustainable, some have argued that NGOs should turn themselves into banks. There is unlikely to be a single answer:

some NGOs may prefer instead to put groups in touch with existing banks so that they are no longer needed. The final element — the assessment of impact — is explored in Chapter 5. This is an area in which there are many methodological difficulties. However, for those interested in poverty reduction, changes in users' livelihoods as a result of microfinance provision are of central importance. The approach proposed is one in which organisations continuously investigate and assess the usefulness and relevance of their services, and adapt their ways of working in response to the results they find. It is suggested that NGOs involved in microfinance should be modest and honest about their aims. Qualitative data gathering which involves users as well as the staff of the microfinance institution can help to clarify how different groups of people — poor, poorest, men, women — are able to make use of the services and with what effect. This information is a vital adjunct to quantitative information on performance, such as numbers of users reached and number and amount of deposits, or volume and size of loans dispersed.

The book makes use of five case studies of financial service schemes connected to or funded by ACTIONAID or Oxfam. In Chapter 6 these schemes are described and used to illustrate issues discussed in earlier chapters in a practical context. Chapter 7 then draws overall conclusions.

1

Current debates in microfinance

1.1 Subsidised credit provision

From the 1950s, governments and international aid donors subsidised credit delivery to small farmers in rural areas of many developing countries. It was assumed that poor people found great difficulty in obtaining adequate volumes of credit and were charged high rates of interest by monopolistic money-lenders. Development finance institutions, such as Agricultural Development Banks, were responsible for the delivery of cheap credit to poor farmers.

These institutions attempted to supervise the uses to which loans were put, and repayment schedules were based on the expected income flow from the investment. Returns were often overestimated. For example, calculations would be based on agricultural yields for good years (Adams and Von Pischke, 1992). As a result, loans were often not repaid. The credibility and financial viability of these subsidised credit schemes were further weakened by the use of public money to waive outstanding and overdue loans at election time (Adams and Von Pischke, 1992; Lipton, 1996; Wiggins and Rogaly, 1989). A dependence on the fluctuating whims of governments and donors, together with poor investment decisions and low repayment rates made many of these development finance institutions unable to sustain their lending programmes. Credit provision for poor people was transitory and limited.

1.2 The move to market-based solutions

This model of subsidised credit was subjected to steady criticism from the mid-1970s as donors and other resource allocators switched attention from state intervention to market-based solutions. Policy-makers were reminded that credit could also be described as debt and that the over-supply of subsidised credit without realistic assessment of people's ability to repay could result in impoverishment for borrowers.

At the same time the concept of 'transaction costs', and the notion that full information about borrowers was not available to lenders, were used by the opponents of subsidised credit to justify the high interest-rates charged by money-lenders. Lending money carries with it the risk of non-repayment. In order to know who is creditworthy and who is not, and so reduce this risk, the lender screens potential borrowers. This involves gathering information on the circumstances of individuals, which may not be easy to obtain. Then enforcement costs are incurred to ensure repayment. Through this process risks are reduced, though not eliminated. Where a loan is disbursed on condition that it is used for a particular purpose, supervision costs also arise.

Using these tools of analysis it was argued that private money-lenders charged interest rates which were higher than formal bank-rates because of the high costs they faced in terms of risk, particularly when lending without physical collateral. At the same time, it was argued that money-lenders were an efficient source of credit because their greater knowledge of the people to whom they were lending lowered screening costs.

Moreover, potential borrowers faced high transaction costs when they sought loans from formal-sector finance institutions. These costs included the time, travel, and paperwork involved in obtaining credit, and were often prohibitive for poor clients, especially those most geographically isolated. On the basis of this analysis, a group of economists based at Ohio State University (USA), notably Dale Adams and J D Von Pischke, put forward the view that the provision of credit should be left almost entirely to the private sector.

In concentrating on the problems of publicly subsidised credit, these economists ignored the social ties, power relations, and coercion associated with the activities of money-lenders. However, detailed micro-level research has demonstrated the widespread use of 'interlocked' contracts to force exchange to the disadvantage of poor people (Bhaduri, 1981). Powerful local people, including landlords, employers, and traders, are able to influence the terms of loans made to tenants, workers, and small producers via conditions set in transactions involving land, labour, or crops. For example, traders frequently lend working capital to small farmers on condition that their crops are sold to that trader at a pre-determined price. Similarly, loans are made to workers against the promise of labour to be provided at below the going rate at a set future date (Rogaly, 1996b).

Against the background of these debates, recent developments in the design of microfinance schemes have generated an understandably high degree of excitement. This is because innovative features in design have reduced the costs and risks of making loans to poor and isolated people, and made financial services available to people who were previously excluded.

1.3 Making use of social collateral

There was little knowledge among formal-sector financial intermediaries of alternatives to physical collateral, until the 1970s, when the Grameen Bank in Bangladesh began using 'peer-group monitoring' to reduce lending risk.

The model for credit delivery in the Grameen Bank is as follows:

- *Groups of five self-select themselves; men's and women's group are kept separate but the members of a single group should have a similar economic background.*

- *Membership is restricted to those with assets worth less than half an acre of land.*

- *Activities begin with savings of Taka 1 per week per person and these savings remain compulsory throughout membership.*

- *Loans are made to two members at a time and must be repaid in equal instalments over 50 weeks.*

- *Each time a loan is taken the borrower must pay 5 per cent of the loan amount into a group fund.*

- *The group is ultimately responsible for repayment if the individual defaults.*

- *Between five and eight groups form a 'development centre' led by a chairperson and secretary and assisted by a Grameen Bank staff member.*

- *Attendance at weekly group and centre meetings is compulsory.*

- *All transactions are openly conducted at centre meetings.*

- *Each member may purchase a share in the Bank worth Taka 100*

Through this system the Grameen Bank has provided credit to over 2 million people in Bangladesh (94 per cent women) with a very low default rate. (Source: Khandker, Khalily and Khan, 1995.)

However, peer-group monitoring has not proved necessary to other institutions seeking to do away with physical collateral. In Indonesia, government-sponsored banks have successfully used character references and locally-recruited lending agents (Chaves and Gonzales Vega, 1996). The peer-group method of Grameen and the individual-user approach of the Bank Rakyat Indonesia (see 1.4) can both be seen as attempts to lower screening costs by using local 'insider' information about the creditworthiness of borrowers. The degree to which Grameen Bank employees themselves implement peer-group monitoring has recently been questioned. It is argued that the reason for the Grameen Bank's high repayment rates is the practice of weekly public meetings at which attendance is compulsory, for the payment of loan instalments and the collection of savings. The meetings reinforce a culture of discipline, routine payments, and staff accountability (Jain, 1996).

Another means of improving loan recovery is to insist on regularity of repayment. This is likely to reflect the actual income-flow of the borrower much better than a lump-sum demand at the end of the loan period. Borrowers can make repayments out of their normal income rather than relying on the returns from a new — often untested — mini-business. Nevertheless, where seasonal agriculture is the main source of income, and borrowers face seasonal hardship, regular repayment scheduling may cause problems.

Microfinance specialists have argued that the prospects for scheme's stability are improved by innovations such as social collateral and regular repayments instalments. Indeed, financial sustainability has become an important goal in itself. To achieve sustainability, microfinance institutions, be they NGOs, government agencies, or commercial banks, need to ensure that the costs of providing the service are kept low and are covered by income earned through interest and fees on loans (see Havers, 1996). As microfinance deals, by definition, with small loans, the income generated through interest payments is also small in comparison with administration costs. To generate profits, therefore, it is necessary to increase scale — in other words, to lend to a large number of people (Otero and Rhyne, 1994).

1.4 Savings

The regular repayments on loans required by large non-governmental microfinance institutions in Bangladesh (including BRAC, ASA and Grameen) provide evidence that poor people can save in cash (Rutherford, 1995a). These intensive repayment regimes are very similar to those of rotating savings and credit associations: steady weekly payments, enforced by social collateral, in return for a lump sum. Loans made are, in reality, advances against this stream of savings.

By insisting on regular savings, microfinance institutions can screen out some potential defaulters, build up the financial security of individuals, increase funds available for lending, and develop among members a degree of identification with the financial health of the institution. People involved in such schemes may previously have been unable to reach formal-sector banks, complete their procedures, qualify for loans or open savings accounts. 'A savings facility is an extremely valuable service in its own right, which often attracts many more clients than a credit programme, particularly from among the poorest' (Hulme and Mosley, 1996, p147).

This evidence that poor people can save in cash has opened up further debate. A distinction is made between schemes in which borrowers must save small and regular amounts in order to obtain loans (termed 'compulsory' saving) and those which offer flexible savings facilities. In the latter case people can deposit and withdraw cash in whatever amounts, and as often, as they wish. This distinction is made especially strongly by Robinson (1995) in her account of the Bank Rakyat Indonesia.

The BRI local banking system has about six times as many deposit accounts as loans. On 31 December 1993, BRI's local banking system had $2.1 billion in deposits. These were all voluntary savings. By 31 December 1995, there were 14.5 million savings accounts. Savers with BRI have access to savings whenever they want.

BRI deals with individuals rather than groups. Its savings programme was designed specifically to meet local demand for security, convenience of location, and choice of savings instruments offering different mixtures of liquidity and returns.

BRI's local banking system has a loan limit of about $11,000. The idea is that good borrowers should not be forced to leave until they can qualify for the loans provided by ordinary commercial banks.

In addition, BRI has a system which gives its borrowers an incentive to repay on time. An additional 25 per cent of the interest rate is added to the monthly payment. This amount is paid back to borrowers at the end of the loan period if they have made every payment in full and on time. There is a corresponding in-built penalty for those who have not. (Source: Robinson, 1994.)

Robinson argues that there is an enormous unmet demand for flexible savings services. However, she also warns that managing a savings system of this type is much more complex than running a simple credit programme.

Schemes which operate under these 'new' savings and credit technologies are an improvement on the old model of subsidised agricultural and micro-enterprise finance. The story of how they have succeeded in reaching poor people is now the subject of a large literature (for example, Rutherford, 1995b; Hulme and Mosley, 1996; Mansell-Carstens, 1995). That many more poor people can now obtain financial services is a major achievement of these schemes. However, the questions of which poor people have been reached, and of whether poverty has been reduced, still remain.

1.5 Can microfinance interventions reduce poverty?

If poverty is understood as low levels of annual income per household, reducing poverty is about raising average income levels. If a particular level of annual income per head is used as a poverty line, poverty reduction could be measured by counting the number or proportion of people who cross that line — who are promoted out of poverty. Providers of financial services who aim to enable people to cross such a poverty line have focused on credit, in particular credit for small enterprises, including agricultural production.

However, attention to annual income can obscure fluctuations in that income during any given year. Poverty can also be understood as vulnerability to downward fluctuations in income. Such fluctuations can be relatively predictable, such as the seasonal decline in employment for agricultural workers, or a shortage of income and trading opportunities in the dry season or before harvest. Alternatively, fluctuations in income may result from unexpected shocks such as crop failure, illness, funeral expenses or loss of an asset such as livestock through theft or death, or a natural disaster such as a cyclone (Montgomery, 1996). Vulnerability can be heightened by the lack of saleable or pawnable assets and by debt obligations. Interventions which reduce such vulnerability and protect livelihoods also reduce poverty.

1.5.1 Poverty as powerlessness

A further dimension of poverty which is often the focus of NGO interventions is powerlessness, whether in an absolute sense or in relation to others. Economic inequality between and within households is likely to be associated with concentrations of political and social power. Inequality can increase whenever better-off people are able to improve their incomes faster than others. Even if the absolute level of material well-being of the worst-off people does not change, relative poverty (Beck, 1994) may increase, and with it a sense of powerlessness among very poor people.

Power relations are partly determined by norms of expected behaviour. Neither the relations nor the norms are static; they are contested and change over time. Powerlessness can be experienced in a variety of situations: within the household, as a result of differences in gender and age; and within the community, between socio-economic groups, as a result of caste, ethnicity, and wealth. Defining poverty in terms of power relations implies that of the impact of microfinance interventions should focus on their influence on social relations and the circumstances which reproduce them. Even in a similar geographical and historical context, it is important to distinguish between the ways in which specific groups of poor people (women and men, landed and landless, particular ethnic groups) are able to benefit from financial services or are excluded from doing so.

1.5.2 Credit for micro-enterprises

While there are methodological difficulties involved in measuring increases in incomes brought about by the provision of credit (see further discussion in Chapter 5), studies have demonstrated that the availability of credit for micro-enterprises can have positive effects. A recent survey collected data from government, NGOs, and banks involved in providing financial services for poor people. Twelve programmes were selected from seven countries (six of these are included in Table 1, Annex 1). Households which had received credit were compared with households which had not. The results demonstrated that credit provision can enable household incomes to rise.

However, taking the analysis further, Hulme and Mosley demonstrated that the better-off the borrower, the greater the increase in income from a micro-enterprise loan. Borrowers who already have assets and skills are able to make better use of credit. The poorest are less able to take risks or use credit to increase their income. Indeed, some of the poorest borrowers interviewed became worse off as a result of micro-enterprise credit, which exposed these vulnerable people to high risks. For them, business failure was more likely to provoke a livelihood crisis than it was for borrowers with a more secure asset base. Specific crises included bankruptcy, forced seizure of assets, and unofficial pledging of assets to other members of a borrowing group. There have even been reports of suicide following peer-group pressure to repay failed loans (Hulme and Mosley, 1996, pp120-122).

A much smaller survey comparing micro-enterprise programmes in El Salvador and Vanuatu found that the development of successful enterprises and the improvement of the incomes of very poor people were conflicting rather than complementary objectives. By selecting those most likely to be successful for credit and training, the programmes inevitably moved away from working with the poorest people (Tomlinson, 1995). Reviews of Oxfam's experiences with income-generating projects for women raised serious questions about the profitability of such activities. Full input costings, which would have revealed many income-generating projects as loss-making, were not carried out. Omissions included depreciation on capital, the opportunity cost of labour (the earnings participants could have had through spending the time on other activities), and subsidisation of income-

11

generating projects with income from other sources. Market research and training in other business skills had often been inadequate (Piza Lopez and March, 1990; Mukhopadhyay and March, 1992).

1.5.3 Reaching the poorest

Whether income promotion is based on loans for individual micro-enterprises or on group-based income generation projects, its appropriateness as a strategy for poverty reduction in the case of the poorest people is questionable. Other evidence suggests that self-selected groups for peer-monitoring have not been inclusive of the poorest people (Montgomery, 1995). People select those with whom they want to form a group on the basis of their own knowledge of the likelihood that these people will make timely payment of loan and savings instalments: X will only have Y in her group if she believes Y is capable of making regular repayments and has much to lose from the social ostracism associated with default. This system might well be expected to lead to the exclusion of the poorest (Montgomery, op. cit.). Even the low asset and land-holding ceiling which the big microfinance institutions in Bangladesh have successfully used to target loans away from better-off people has not necessarily meant that the poorest, who are often landless, are included (Osmani, 1989).

So while the innovations referred to earlier appear to have made loans more available to poor people, there is still debate over the design of appropriate financial services for the poorest. Hulme and Mosley's study strongly suggests that providing credit for micro-enterprises is unlikely to help the poorest people to increase their incomes. However, detailed research with users has found that some design features of savings and credit schemes are able to meet the needs of very poor people. For example, it was found that easy access to savings and the provision of emergency loans by SANASA (see 3.4.2) enabled poor people to cope better with seasonal income fluctuations (Montgomery, 1996).

Microfinance specialists increasingly, therefore, view improvements in economic security — income protection rather than promotion (Dreze and Sen, 1989) — as the first step in poverty reduction. '...from the perspective of *poverty reduction*, access to reliable, monetized savings facilities can help the poor smooth consumption over periods of cyclical or unexpected crises, thus greatly improving their economic security.' It is only when people have some economic security that 'access to credit can help them move out of poverty by improving the productivity of their enterprises or creating new sources of livelihood' (Bennet and Cuevas, 1996, authors' emphasis).

1.6 Financial interventions and social change

Interventions have an impact on social relations partly through their economic effects. In many instances implementors of credit schemes have claimed that the work will lead to progressive social change, for example by empowering women and changing gender relations in the household and in the community (Ackerly, 1995). In five out of the six schemes summarised in Table 1 (Annex 1), over half of the borrowers were women.

Much of the work that has been done in assessing the impact of credit programmes on women has been in Bangladesh. One approach was to look at the control women retained over loans extended to them by four different credit programmes: the Grameen Bank, BRAC, a large government scheme (the Rural Poor Programme RD-12), and a small NGO (Thangemara Mahila Senbuj Sengstha) (Goetz and Sen Gupta, 1996). Results suggested that women retained significant control over the use to which the loan was put in 37 per cent of cases; 63 per cent fell into the categories of partial, limited or no control over loan use. Goetz and Sen Gupta found single, divorced, and widowed women more likely to retain control than others. Control was also retained more often when loan sizes were small and when loan use was based on activities which did not challenge notions of appropriate work for women and men. The question of whether women were empowered is not answered: even when they did not control loans, they may have used the fact that the loan had been disbursed to them as women to increase their status and strengthen their position in the household. However, in some cases women reported an increase in domestic violence because of disputes over cash for repayment instalments.

A second major piece of research has assessed the effect of Grameen and BRAC programmes on eight indicators of women's empowerment: mobility, economic security, ability to make small purchases, ability to make larger purchases, involvement in major household decisions, relative freedom from domination by the family, political and legal awareness, and participation in public protests and political campaigning (Hashemi *et al*, 1996). The study concludes that, on balance, access to credit has enabled women to negotiate within the household to improve their position. However, unlike the Goetz and Sen Gupta study, which is based on 275 detailed loan-use histories, Hashemi *et al* attempted to compare villages where Grameen or BRAC were present with villages where they were not. Because of difficulties inherent in finding perfect control villages (which the authors acknowledge), the conclusions of the study do not signify the end of the debate.

It has also been argued that focusing on women is much more to do with financial objectives than with the aim of empowerment. According to

13

Rutherford (1995b) the real reasons for targeting women in Bangladesh are that they are seen as accessible (being at home during working hours); more likely to repay on time; more pliable and patient than men; and cheaper to service (as mainly female staff can be hired).

Thus the process of loan supervision and recovery may be deliberately internalised inside the household (Goetz and Sen Gupta, op. cit.). Goetz and Sen Gupta do not use this as an argument against the provision of finance for women in Bangladesh, but rather suggest that to avoid aggravating gender-based conflict, loans should be given to men directly as well as to women and, at the same time, that efforts should be made to change men's attitudes to women's worth.

1.7 Treading carefully in microfinance interventions

This brief summary of evidence and argument suggests that microfinance interventions may increase incomes, contribute to individual and household livelihood security, and change social relations for the better. But that they can not always be assumed to be doing so. Financial services are not always the most appropriate intervention. The poorest, in particular, often face pressing needs in terms of primary health care, education, and employment opportunities. Lipton has recently argued for anti-poverty resources to be allocated across sectors on the basis that a concentration on a single intervention mechanism, say credit, is much less effective in poverty reduction than simultaneous credit, primary health, and education work, even if this entails narrowing geographical focus (op. cit.). The particular combinations which will be most effective will depend on the nature of poverty in a specific context. Although microfinance provision appears to be evolving towards greater sustainability, relevance, and usefulness, there are few certainties and the search for better practice continues.

Decisions on whether and how to intervene in local financial markets should not be taken without prior knowledge of the working of those markets. If the intervention is intended to reduce poverty, it is especially important to know the degree to which poor people use existing services and on what terms. Only then can an intervening agency or bank make an informed decision on whether their work is likely to augment or displace existing 'pro-poor' financial services. If the terms of informal financial transactions are likely to work against the interests of poor people (cases in which the stereotype of 'the wicked money-lender' corresponds to reality) the intervention may attempt to compete with and possibly replace part of the informal system. However, making such an informed assessment is not straightforward, as one study of the power relations between informal financial service providers and agricultural producers in Tamil Nadu demonstrated. Grain merchants based in the market town of Dindigul were found to dictate the terms of product sale when lending working capital to very small-scale farmers, but to be much the weaker party when lending to larger-scale farmers (Rogaly, 1985).

The structure of a credit market can change, partly under the influence of outside intervention. Rutherford has studied the changing market in financial services for poor people in Bangladesh. Competition between NGOs is leading to users being less subservient to NGO staff and protesting about unpopular financial obligations, such as the 5 per cent deducted from loans by Grameen for a 'group fund'. Private individuals have set up offices imitating the Grameen style but charging higher interest rates on loans than the big NGOs, and also offering higher rates on savings deposits. Private urban finance companies have expanded. Despite the tendency for NGOs to become more like banks, other formal-sector lenders are still reluctant to lend to poor people (see also McGregor, 1994).

The expansion of NGO credit in Bangladesh has been made possible by the flood of donor money to that country. One study of BRAC showed that loan disbursal and recovery had become more important than group formation (Montgomery, 1996). In 1992, Grameen Bank and BRAC employees were found to be offering 'immediate loans' to women in villages where smaller NGOs had been attempting longer-term group-based finance (Ebdon, 1995). Ebdon attributed this behaviour to fairly strict targets for loan disbursal in the case of BRAC, and in both cases to an imperative for job security for staff and a desire on the part of the organisations to expand their influence and strengthen their reputations (p52).

This anxiety to increase the number of users can undercut the very basis of the new model: the creation of sustainable financial institutions. Studies of credit schemes have consistently demonstrated that unless borrowers and savers believed they would benefit from the long-term survival of the institution, and have a sense of ownership, repayment rates would decline (Rogaly, 1991; Copestake, 1996a). The sense of ownership is weakened by attempts by large microfinance institutions in Bangladesh to claim territory by encroachment. In India, in the absence of equivalent flows of external finance, thrift and credit co-operatives based much more on borrowers' requirements have emerged (Rutherford, 1995b, p136). An understanding of the way in which the institutions themselves change and respond to incentives is therefore necessary for the design of relevant anti-poverty interventions, including financial services.

2

Informal financial services

2.1 Introduction

In recent years research into informal financial services and systems has significantly deepened understanding of the way they operate and their strengths and weaknesses. A simplistic belief that local money-lenders charged extortionate interest rates lay behind the provision of subsidised finance in the past. More thorough investigation has highlighted a range of savings, credit, and insurance facilities accessible to poor people. The apparently usurious interest charges reportedly made by private money-lenders may be explainable in terms of transaction costs, lack of information, and high risk. Informal financial services may be well-equipped, because of local 'insider' knowledge, and lower overheads, to respond to the requirements of poor people; they may also be exploitative.

This chapter starts with a brief overview of the types of informal services that have been found to exist in a wide variety of countries and social contexts.[1] Some of the broad characteristics of these services are identified, and lessons drawn for the design of NGO or semi-formal systems. In describing informal financial services it is useful to distinguish between those which are owned by their users and those which are offered by an individual, usually on a profit-making basis. The distinction can be a helpful one in analysing the ways in which financial services enable or exploit poor people.

NGOs considering microfinance interventions need first to find out what informal financial services are available, and how they operate. Such services are capable of supporting poor people's livelihoods as well as perpetuating

---

1 This chapter draws heavily on a background paper commissioned for the purposes of this book: *A Critical Typology of Financial Services for the Poor,* Stuart Rutherford, November 1996. Examples are drawn from Rutherford's own experience unless otherwise stated.

structures which undermine them. It is necessary, therefore, to understand under what circumstances and to what degree these services are enabling or exploitative for poor people. On the whole, user-owned services are likely to be more enabling than services provided for profit.

Investigating the scope and nature of existing services is an essential preliminary before considering whether an intervention is necessary. However, NGOs themselves may not have the right skills to become direct providers of financial services. Furthermore, financial services are needed by poor people on a permanent basis to enable them to plan and manage their finances; NGO programmes which might be here today and gone tomorrow may be an inappropriate means through which to provide them. Therefore NGOs should seriously consider whether direct intervention is in fact the best response for them to make. The chapter closes by discussing alternative strategies NGOs might employ.

2.2 User-owned informal financial services

Systems which facilitate financial transactions and are owned by their users are many and varied, and range from simple reciprocal arrangements between neighbours, savings clubs and rotating savings and credit associations (ROSCAs), to forms of insurance, building societies, and systems of co-operative business finance. An example of each of these types is described below. All of these systems can be found in a variety of country settings.

Rotating savings and credit associations (ROSCAs) in particular, are an extremely common phenomenon. They exist in almost every country (for example, 'partners' in Jamaica and Britain, *hui* in Vietnam, and *njangi* in Cameroon). (See Bouman, 1995; Ardener and Burman, 1995 for detailed and extensive surveys of ROSCA operations in a range of settings.) The principle is very simple: a number of people agree to save a fixed amount of money at regular intervals; at each meeting, for example weekly, each member contributes an agreed amount, resulting in a single lump sum becoming available, which is then allocated to one of the members. There are three basic variations in the way in which this lump sum or 'prize' is allocated. First, it can be allocated on the basis of strict rotation between members of the group; second, on the basis of a lottery of members; third, it may be auctioned to the member who is willing to accept the biggest discount. The group will usually meet (but does not always need to) and undertake this transaction on as many occasions as there are members of the group, thus ensuring that each member gets the 'prize' once. The ROSCA demonstrates the basic principle of financial intermediation: collecting many small savings from many people, turning this into a lump sum for one person, and repeating this procedure over time.

ROSCA finance is used for many purposes. Some ROSCAs operate to enable an asset to be purchased, such as a rickshaw or fishing equipment for each member, and may have been set up specifically for the purpose. 'Merry-go-rounds', as ROSCAs are called among Kikuyu women in Kenya, are sometimes used by women as a means of accumulating enough money to buy new household utensils or clothes. The technology of the ROSCA is not unique to poor communities but is also used by salaried professionals to purchase major consumption items or assets such as refrigerators or cars.

A further example of a user-owned device is the insurance fund which makes pay-outs conditional on certain circumstances occurring. These are intended to cover large expenses such as those connected with marriage or death.

2.2.1 Some examples of user-owned financial services

Neighbourhood reciprocity in Southern India

Reciprocal lending may be extended to involve several or even all the members of a community. Among Moslems in Kerala State in southern India kuri kalyanam *are invitations to a feast to which the guest is expected to bring a cash gift. When the host in his turn is invited to a feast by one of the guests he is expected to return double the amount (less if he is perceived as poor). In Vietnam one kind of* hui *(a generic name for various financial devices) involves a similar pooling of resources for one person on one occasion to be reciprocated later by others, at different times.*

Rickshaw ROSCAs in Bangladesh

Very poor men driven by poverty from their home villages to the Bangladesh capital, Dhaka, often earn a living there by driving hired rickshaws. In the last ten years they have begun to run ROSCAs. A group of drivers forms, and each driver saves a set amount from his daily takings. When the fund is large enough (this usually takes about 15 days) a rickshaw is bought and distributed by lottery to one of the members. In between 'prizes' the cash is held by a trustworthy outsider, usually a local shopkeeper from whom the members buy their tea or cigarettes. In a further adaptation, those who have already received their rickshaw double their daily contribution. This progressively reduces the time-gap between prizes, and is seen as a fair way of rewarding those members who win the lottery late in the cycle, because their gross contribution is smaller than earlier winners. The extra payment made by the winners is roughly equivalent to what they save by no longer having to hire a rickshaw.

An accumulating savings club in Mexico

In towns and villages in Mexico neighbours place frequent but irregular savings with trusted shopkeepers. Just before Christmas, the cash is returned to the saver. No interest is paid, but the saver has a lump sum to spend, and the shopkeeper has had the use of the money over the year and can now look forward to a good sales season.

Building societies for the middle classes in Bangladesh

In a lower-middle-class area of Dhaka, 165 employees in the Public Works Department belong to their own 'building society' which was started over 16 years ago. Each saves 200 taka ($5) a month out of his wages. As the cash accumulates it is lent out to members, who buy land and building materials. Interest rates are high and interest on the outstanding balance has to be paid each month, to encourage modest loans and rapid repayment. But loan sizes are generous and such workers would have few or no alternative sources for loans of this kind.

Popular insurance: funeral funds (iddir) in Ethiopia

Originally burial societies, iddir have extended to provide a wide range of insurance services in urban Ethiopia. Aredo (1993), studying these in Addis Ababa, estimated that 50 per cent of urban households were members of some kind of iddir. Groups of people come together on the basis of location, occupation, friendship or family ties. Each iddir sets its own rules and regulations but usually pays out for funeral expenses or financial assistance to families of the deceased, and sometimes to cover other costs, such as medical expenses and losses due to fire or theft.

2.3 Informal financial services for profit

Those offering informal financial services for profit fall into two groups: deposit takers (often also called money-guards) and lenders.

What is most interesting about the situation of deposit takers is that, as in the Nigerian example below, savers usually pay for the service by obtaining a negative interest rate on their funds. This demonstrates the pressing need that people have for places to put their savings which are safe and secure not only from physical risks such as theft, fire or flood, but also from the demands of their family. For women, in particular, the ability to save small amounts in places to which their husbands and families cannot gain access (although they might know about them) has been shown to be particularly important. It may enable them to meet obligations in the family or household, such as the payment of children's school fees, for which they have particular responsibility.

Forms of lending also operate in a variety of ways, such as money-lenders; pawnbrokers, who take collateral in the form of physical assets; and forms of trade credit and hire purchase. The term 'money-lender' can cause confusion because it conjures up the image of a class of people whose main source of income is usury. In reality, many small farmers, for example, obtain credit from employers, landlords, traders, relatives, and other people who combine a number of economic activities. In some places money-lenders may be a more professionalised class, such as the 'Tamilians' in Cochin described below, but even in this case it is not necessarily their main source of income.

Lending money can be *exploitative* of, as well as *enabling* for, poor people. People facing seasonal shortages may have only one source of credit, for example, an employer. The employer may agree to provide a loan, but only if the borrower promises to work when required at below the going wage-rate. As described below for Indonesia, crop traders may provide producers with seasonal credit on the understanding that the crop is sold through the same trader at low post-harvest prices. Tied credit of this type, whether in cash or kind, may be the only means of survival for poor people. But arrangements such as these can maintain and even exacerbate inequalities in power and position. In contrast, user-owned devices are likely to be more supportive and enabling, because the profits made are pooled, and shared or fed back into the system, and ownership and control of the funds are in the hands of the users. Such devices are unlikely to be exploitative of those involved, although they may widen inequalities between users and non-users. The comparison with services for profit is clear.

However, loans from private lenders after harvest may enable small traders to make the most of the increased liquidity in the local economy. This emphasises the need for interveners to understand the workings of real markets and to question untested assumptions. It is essential to find out for which groups of poor people — women, men, landless labourers, subsistence farmers, migrant workers — and under what circumstances these arrangements may be no more than a means of survival, while supporting wealth creation for others.

2.3.1 Some examples of informal financial services provided for profit

Deposit takers: a mobile **alajo** *in Nigeria*
One consequence of Nigeria's current political difficulties is a drop in public confidence in formal banks, according to Gemini News. This has allowed an old tradition to flourish again — alajos, or peripatetic deposit takers. Idowu Alakpere uses a bicycle to go

*door-to-door round the outer suburb of Lagos where he lives. He has
500 customers who each save about 10 or 15 naira with him (about
50 to 75 cents US) at each daily visit. Customers withdraw money
whenever they like, and Idowu charges them one day's savings per
month, which he deducts from the withdrawal. Since deposits are
made evenly over the month, the negative interest rate for one-month
deposits is 1/15, or 6.6 per cent a month, an Annual Percentage Rate
(APR) of 80 per cent. Some* alajos, *including Idowu, store the cash
in a reliable bank, others use it to make loans. The* Gemini News
reporter was told by many local people that they trusted these alajos
more than banks. When it was pointed out that some alajos *are
dishonest, they retorted that so are many banks.*

Professional money-lenders in Cochin, India
*'Tamilians' provide a money-lending service to poor slum dwellers
on a daily basis. They have set terms, which are well-known all over
Cochin. For each 100 rupees lent, 3 rupees are deducted at source as
a fee. Thereafter, 12.50 rupees per week must be repaid for ten weeks.
This works out at an APR of 300 per cent (28 rupees paid on an
average size loan of 48.50 rupees [97/2] for 10/52 of a year). Most
non-poor observers regard this rate as outrageously exploitative.
However, poor users of the service tend to take a favourable view of
it. The 'Tamilians' do not needlessly harass their clients over repayment but take an 'understanding' view which includes a willingness
to accept loan losses. These money-lenders know their clients well
and (out of self-interest) will not lend more than they think the
client can repay out of normal income over the next ten weeks.*

Lending against collateral: pawnbrokers in Western India
*Residents of the slums of Vijayawada use their local pawnbroker
when they need money quickly. He is reliably available at his gold-
smithing shop and he charges 3 per cent a month for loans pledged
against gold, 5 per cent for silver and 9 per cent for brass. The inclu-
sion of brass means that even the very poor can get a small advance
by pawning kitchen pots and pans. He lends up to two-thirds the
value of the pawn. He gives a receipt, and because the borrower can
be sure of getting her pawn back when she repays the loan, she can
risk pawning objects of sentimental value. Unlike those who lend
without collateral the broker does not need to know his clients well:
the unambiguous collateral provided by the pawn means that the
broker can lend to more or less anyone at any time.*

Advance crop sales in Indonesia
A practice common in many countries is known as ijon *in some areas of Indonesia. Farmers often need cash to get them through the 'hungry' season when their main crop is in the ground and there is not much else to do except sit and wait. They are forced to make an advance sale of the crop, usually to a grain buyer or his agent. Ijon transactions of this sort, if seen as loans, show an interest rate of anything from 10 to 40 per cent a month.*
(Source: Bouman and Moll in Adams and Fitchett, 1992.)

Two examples of trade credit
In many markets it is common to see poor people squatting on the ground with a small amount of fertiliser spread out on a mat. The fertiliser doesn't necessarily belong to the man or woman (or, often, child). Lacking capital themselves to buy stock, such people obtain the fertiliser on credit from a nearby shop. At the close of the market they return the money from sales and any balance of the stock to the shopkeeper, retaining a small proportion of the money. The system allows people to trade (safely if not profitably) without capital, and gives the shopkeeper a cheap extra outlet.

The dadon *credit system used to finance prawn cultivation in Bangladesh is an example of a trading system in which credit is passed on through a chain of intermediaries between the prawn farmer and exporters to Europe. The prawn market is a highly competitive business in which everyone in the chain is short of capital. The 'commission agent' at the port buys prawns on behalf of the exporters in the capital. To ensure their share of the market they provide credit early in the season which finds its way through a number of intermediaries before reaching the hands of the farmer. The intermediaries are 'depot' owners, then 'farias', or merchants, and finally local traders, who in turn lend to the farmers. In accepting the credit the farmer commits himself to selling exclusively to this particular trader.*

2.4 Turning the informal into the formal

In some countries such informal systems have evolved into formal systems which have had a major impact on their users. In the UK, for example, 'mutual' or friendly societies which began as small thrift groups in the nineteenth century turned into building societies in the first half of the twentieth, and have been the main source of housing finance for 50 years.

There are further examples of such informal systems becoming increasingly formalised. Aredo (1993) reports that the *iddir* in Addis Ababa run by the Ethiopia Teachers' Association is of the scale of a medium-size insurance business. In Cameroon some of the traditional ROSCAs known as *njangi* have evolved into small banks offering finance for small businesses which have difficulty using formal banks (Haggblade, 1978). ROSCAs may thus be a transitional phenomenon.

Chit funds in India are a formalised version of a ROSCA, for which government legislation exists. In contrast to the ROSCA, members of the chit fund do not normally know each other and are merely customers of the chit companies. The company advertises for and selects members, makes arrangements for collection of subscriptions, and holds auctions for the prizes. However, such funds are of limited use to poor people, who lack both the income to pay subscriptions and the social position to gain the confidence of the company.

The transition to formalised services is not inevitable. Informal and formal arrangements continue to exist side-by-side even in industrialised countries. In Oxford, UK,ROSCAs have enabled people with very limited capital of their own to increase their chances of obtaining a small business loan (Srinivasan, 1995).

A detailed comparative study of credit use among low-income Pakistani, Bangladeshi, and Carribean immigrants in the UK revealed enormous differences in their use of financial services. In all cases sources of credit were classified into high-street credit, local commercial credit, mail order, social fund, community-based credit, and 'miscellaneous' (including friends, family, and employer). Unlike the Bangladeshis, the Pakistani and Carribean respondents reported community-based, ROSCA-like arrangements. Bangladeshi respondents made much more use of formal bank credit than the others, although they had at least as high a proportion of applications rejected, apparently on racial grounds (Herbert and Kempson, 1996).

Abugre (1994) points out that transition and change can be rapid, discontinuous, and turbulent rather than smooth and linear. There is therefore likely to be a multiplicity of arrangements, some of which become formalised, while others die out, and yet others are initiated. The implication for those interested in providing financial services is that such a role must be carefully thought through, and be flexible and responsive to changing circumstances.

2.5 What can be learned from informal finance?

Having briefly explored the range of financial services which may exist, it is clear that informal finance is a regular feature of poor people's lives. What can be learned from this? The continuation of a large number of different forms suggest the following points (partly adapted from Adams, 1992).

There is clearly a demand for financial services
The range of informal financial services available partly reflects
the varied requirements which people, both rich and poor, have for
financial services. They may also be explained in terms of the actions
of people with excess cash seeking to earn income from lending. In
some cases, especially where there is a monopoly, or collusion among
providers, this can be exploitative for the borrower. Informal services
available include savings facilities, provision of credit for consumption,
and funding for predictable but expensive events such as marriages
and funerals. This is in significant contrast to the services that NGOs
have generally offered, which have usually been limited to the
provision of credit for production.

Transaction costs are low.
Transaction costs are the costs, other than interest payments, which
are incurred in making a deposit or taking a loan. They include travel,
time away from other activities, related 'gifts' which might have to be
offered to bank or government officials, costs in obtaining documentation required, such as land certificates, and so on. Compared to formal
services, local informal services generally require very little form-filling
or travel. However, the advantage to the borrower of low transaction
costs may be more than counterbalanced by their lack of power in
setting the terms of a loan, which may be exploitative.

Informal services impose their own discipline.
The flow of information locally and the small number of providers
of informal finance often act as powerful incentives to users to repay
loans or save in a disciplined way. A ROSCA member failing to pay
their instalment risks social ostracism from neighbours, friends, and
relatives; they may be less likely to receive help from these people
in times of severe difficulty in future.

Poor people are capable of saving
The evidence of informal systems disproves the assumption that
poor people cannot save. Saving 'in kind' has long been a recognised
part of people's livelihood management: saving in cash is a necessity of
interaction with the cash economy. Indeed it is often the poorest, who
are landless or for other reasons dependent on casual, poorly-paid jobs,
who gain a large proportion of their incomes in cash and therefore have
most need of savings facilities. The evidence shows that poor people
are not only willing to save but at present often pay highly
for savings facilities.

Informal systems are adaptable.
The variety of forms and functions of informal finance demonstrates the adaptability of these systems to different economic conditions and changing circumstances. This contrasts with formal systems which often have to be based on a uniform delivery model.

There is thus much to be learned from informal financial systems. Indeed aspects of these systems have found their way into the design of NGO and semi-formal financial services programmes. In particular, both group-based and individual-based schemes have made use of the 'insider knowledge' of other local people: individual-based schemes, such as BRI, through personal references from local representatives, and group-based schemes, such as Grameen, through self-selecting groups of borrowers (see Chapter 1).

This brief overview has not identified *for whom* these services exist — women and men, poor or poorest. The poorest people may find it difficult to save the amount that a ROSCA requires and hence find participation a burden or are excluded. Even if there are a number of people in similar situations, they are often marginalised or isolated and lack the social networks to create their own ROSCA with a lower fee. Indebtedness may also make it difficult for the poorest to save and build up a small asset base — a situation that will be illustrated in the case of low-income and unemployed members of the Ladywood Credit Union in the UK, a case-study scheme described in Chapter 6. There are therefore limitations to the extent to which savings-based user-owned facilities can be of use to very poor people. However, systems that allow flexible amounts to be deposited are more likely to be appropriate.

2.6 Deciding when and how to intervene

Before going on to discuss ways of intervening which are useful and relevant to poor people (see Chapter 3), it is necessary to issue some warnings. Several commentators, among them NGO practitioners, have questioned the appropriateness of NGOs acting as providers of financial services. Abugre (1992) identifies a range of dangers, and points to the dire consequences of the job being done badly:

- NGOs remain averse to charging positive real interest rates and may, consciously or otherwise, undermine traditional financial systems.

- NGOs do not submit themselves to the discipline required for the provision of sustainable financial services.

● Schemes are managed by entirely unprofessional and untrained staff and are often carelessly conceived, designed, and implemented.

● There are cases where NGOs have flooded the market with credit, resulting in indebtedness on the part of borrowers, and potentially regressive effects on income and wealth distribution. By extending loans which poor people are unable to pay due to factors beyond their control, or which may have simply been inappropriate in the first place, NGOs can cause a level of indebtedness which may result in the borrower having to liquidate assets in order to repay.

Abugre therefore warns against the hasty introduction of new financial services by NGOs and concludes that they should concentrate on what they do well, such as providing social services and acting as confidence brokers in communities.

Direct provision may be a risky and problematic strategy for an NGO, particularly as the NGO may not have the range of skills required to develop microfinance interventions, nor experience of the financial skills and responsibility required to ensure funds are properly safeguarded and accounted for. A further range of managerial skills are also necessary in managing a portfolio of financial assets such as loans and deposits. NGOs with experience of welfare and relief have more experience of channelling funds than managing them (Bouman, 1995). An NGO must ask itself whether it has the skills to become a banker.

An organisation lacking the relevant skills may consider acquiring them either through recruitment or staff development. Such a strategy itself has important consequences. These skills may be in short supply and recruitment prove difficult; they take time to develop and are acquired through experience as well as training. There is often a strong impetus to start work even if the skills of staff are still weak. This can endanger the intervention itself since it is at this early stage that users gain an impression of the nature of the operation, and inexperienced staff are likely to make mistakes.

Embarking on direct intervention also raises questions about the long-term sustainability of the service on offer. Financial services should not be provided on a transient or temporary basis. There needs to be a degree of permanence to enable people to plan for their future financial needs. Consideration of the long-term future for a system of financial service provision is therefore important at the outset. Direct provision by an NGO which expects to move away from the area would seldom be appropriate.

There is a further range of issues at the level of the macro-economy which should also be considered when deciding whether to intervene. Macro-economic stability is an important pre-requisite for getting a scheme off the ground.[2] Hyper-inflation and economic instability do not encourage individuals to save, and loans under such circumstances are difficult to manage. (However, in Mexico, while formal-sector banks were reeling from massive default caused by the high interest rates and high inflation of 1995, URAC, one of the case-study institutions discussed in Chapter 6, continued to thrive.) Political stability is also needed, since without it there is unlikely to be much confidence in the long-term future of new financial institutions. Before considering scheme design an NGO must also investigate the formal legal regulatory requirements for organisations involved in financial service provision, especially for savings (see Chapter 3).

2.6.1 Research questions on existing informal financial services

In carrying out research into the services available, and how they are used, an intervener should try to find answers to a wide range of questions, such as:

How do people manage their savings deposits?
Are there savings banks, or deposit takers, insurance salesmen, or savings clubs? Do poor people have access to them? If not, how do they save (for example, gold, livestock). Who among the poor uses them (men, women, landless labourers, subsistence farmers etc)?

(Extensive use of expensive deposit takers might indicate that the NGO should look first at the reasons why alternatives are not in place: and second at whether there is any possibility for the NGO to get involved, either as promoter or as provider, in savings collection.)

How do people temporarily realise the value of assets they hold?
Are there pawnbrokers or are there schemes that allow them to pawn land or other major assets (eg jewellery) safely? Who uses these services?

(If such devices exist, are they exploitative or enabling? If they are clearly exploitative, there might be a case for an NGO to try to provide or promote an alternative.)

How do people get access to the current value of future savings?
Are there money-lenders willing to advance small loans against future savings? Are there ROSCAs or managed or commercial chits, or co-operative

---

2 In a background paper commissioned for the purposes of this book, Shahin Yaqub examined the 'Macroeconomic Conditions for Successful Microfinance for Poor People'. The paper is available from the Policy Department, Oxfam (UK and Ireland).

banks? Do poor people have access? Which poor people use them? (If money-lenders appear to be exploiting users, for example by imposing very high interest rates or linking loans to disadvantageous deals over land, labour or commodities, then there might be a case for the NGO to introduce ROSCAs or annual savings clubs, or work as a promoter of self-help groups or credit unions.)

How do people make provision for known life-cycle expenses?
Do they provide for daughters' marriages, their own old age and funeral, for their heirs? Are there clubs that satisfy these needs, or general savings services or insurance companies that will do as well? Are there government or employer-run schemes? Are there particular expenses for which women have responsibility?

How do people cope with emergencies?
What happens when a breadwinner is ill, or when a flood or drought occurs? Does the government have schemes that reach poor people in these circumstances? If not, what local provision do people make?

How do small-scale entrepreneurs get access to business finance?
If so, in what amounts and at what cost? Do women entrepreneurs have access?

During the exploratory work done to answer these questions another set of information will come to light — the absolute quantities of cash involved in local financial intermediation. This can be of immense value to scheme designers in cases where a decision is made to intervene. For example, information about amounts repaid regularly to money-lenders will be useful in setting loan sizes and repayment schedules for loan schemes. (Source: Rutherford, 1996.)

Much can be learned from the way in which people are already managing their finances. A further aspect is the social relations involved — the groups of people who get together to form ROSCAs, those from whom loans are taken, and those with whom deposits are lodged. Tierney's work on the Oxfam-funded Youth Employment Groups in Tabora Region of Tanzania demonstrates that the design of the intervention, which was based around groups of people with the same occupational background, did not correspond to the pattern of existing financial intermediation, which was organised around small kin-based groups, each including diverse enterprises. Tierney argues that 'the formation of development groups can, ironically, divert people's energy away from improving their lives, because forming the kind of groups which are eligible for financial assistance is a time-consuming activity involving skill in manipulating and maintaining public relations' (Tierneyforthcoming).This illustrates the value of understanding how indigenous financial systems operate, before designing a new microfinance initiative.

2.7 Filling the gaps

As well as alerting people to the potential pitfalls of intervention, research to answer the kind of questions suggested above is likely to identify gaps in existing services. There are many ways in which such gaps can be filled and below are some examples of financial service interventions in insurance and hire purchase which can be of use to poor people. For those agencies whose motivation is poverty reduction it is important to link the identification of gaps with a poverty analysis to determine who is excluded from existing services and how such exclusion perpetuates poverty.

2.7.1 Some examples of innovative services

Hire-then-purchase for the poor in Bangladesh
ACTIONAID found, through the experience of running a group-based lending programme similar to that of the Grameen Bank, that many very poor people were nervous of taking a large loan — the 5,000 taka ($125) needed to buy a rickshaw, for example — in case they were not able to repay it. AA therefore devised a hire-then-purchase scheme for such people. AA bought its own rickshaws and hired them out to group members. A rickshaw driver could hire a rickshaw from AA instead of hiring one from a local 'mohajan'. If he then decided to convert his contract with AA from hiring to buying, a proportion of the total hiring fees he had already paid was denoted as his down-payment, and he took a regular (smaller) AA loan to pay off the rest.

Door-step insurance agents, Cuttack, Orissa
In Cuttack, insurance agents from the Peerless company visit households in low-income areas. They offer simple endowment schemes, which from the point of view of the customers are like accumulating fixed deposit schemes: the customer puts in a fixed amount regularly and then on maturity gets it back plus profits. Life insurance cover is included in the contract.

'Bankassurance': group-based insurance for the rural poor
In Bangladesh, one insurance company is pioneering an attempt to match, in the field of insurance, Grameen Bank's success in lending.

Delta Life Insurance has been experimenting since 1988 with cut-price basic life-insurance for rural people. Customers are arranged in groups, there is no medical examination and no age-bar, and premiums are tiny and collected weekly. Agents are also involved in Grameen-Bank-style lending and earn an extra commission for the insurance work. In fact the insurance premiums are invested directly in lending (on which healthy interest may be earned). In 1996 Delta was looking for a big NGO partner which could offer the two services — lending and insurance — side by side. Experience so far has shown that demand for such a service is high. Delta is exploring how it can extend this initiative beyond life insurance.

2.8 Promotion: an alternative strategy for NGOs

Having identified the gaps in existing financial service provision, an NGO might involve itself in *promotion* rather than provision. The main alternatives to direct provision of financial services are ones which involve the NGO in a transitional or support role whereby activities such as mobilisation, training, and making links to other organisations are provided. A range of possible approaches are outlined.

2.8.1 Formation of savings groups and development of internal credit facilities

Where ROSCAs do not exist or have limited coverage, the NGO might act as a facilitator of their formation or enable them to develop slightly more sophisticated systems of internal on-lending which allows savings and loans to take on more flexible formats. This approach has been used by Friends of Women's World Banking in India. In this case the NGO is mainly involved in training and organising the groups.

Self-help groups (SHGs) are NGO-led attempts to promote savings clubs, or simple forms of credit union. Those initiated by Friends of Women's World Banking in India are aimed at poor rural women. FWWB (or its partner NGOs) persuades women from the same neighbourhood and from similar backgrounds to form small groups of 12 to 15 members. NGO workers encourage the women to meet regularly and frequently and during these meetings the women discuss their financial problems and ways of solving them.

The solution they are steered towards involves regular small savings and the immediate conversion of those savings into small loans taken by one or two members at each meeting. Care is taken to involve all group members in the discussion and formulation of rules (how often to meet, the interest to be charged on loans, and repayment arrangements) and then to ensure that every member experiences for herself the activities of saving and of taking and repaying a loan.

The group is asked to choose leaders who are trained to manage the group's affairs: if illiteracy or very poor educational levels are a problem then rules are kept deliberately simple (fixed equal savings, and annual dividends rather than monthly interest on savings, for example). These preparations are intended to equip the group for independent survival after the NGO stops sending workers regularly to the meetings. Groups which perform well over several months are able to obtain small bulk loans made by FWWB to the group as a collective. Where there are a number of groups in an area, FWWB may help them form a 'federation' ('apex body') to help with liquidity problems: groups with excess savings deposit them with the federation which on-lends to groups with a strong demand for loans.
(Source: WWB, 1993.)

However, although this type of intervention can succeed with agency help, it has yet to be proved whether savings and credit groups which are promoted by outsiders can achieve long-term independence (Rutherford, 1996). A range of questions remain: can they save sufficient funds among themselves to satisfy their own demand for loans? Can external funds be introduced into these groups without destroying their independence?

2.8.2 Promotion of small-scale formalised approaches

National legislation may allow for credit unions (the World Council of Credit Unions has national and regional affiliates all over the world) or thrift and credit co-operatives (as in Sri Lanka, see 3.4.2). Another approach an NGO might adopt could be the linking up of people interested in establishing such services for themselves with other credit unions or umbrella and apex bodies that are able to promote and advise on particular financial services.

Oxfam Hyderabad worked with the Federation of Thrift and Credit Associations in Andhra Pradesh, encouraging exposure visits to flourishing thrift and credit societies by potential members from other areas. The members now have a source of consumption credit based on their own savings. Oxfam Hyderabad saw its support for linking potential groups with an existing thrift and credit structure as a move away from direct funding of NGOs to provide credit.
(Source: Oxfam (India) Trust, 1993.)

2.8.3 Linking groups to the formal system

Existing savings groups or ROSCAs may already have bank savings accounts but are unable to take loans because the bank does not understand their operations or believe them to be creditworthy. The NGO might work with groups to encourage them to build up savings and deposit them in formal institutions. The NGO may then be able to work with a local bank to encourage it to extend its services to groups.

In Ghana, rural banking legislation was designed to create semi-autonomous local banks which would serve people cut off from financial services. However, the banks have experienced a range of problems which led to only 23 out of a total of 123 being classified as operating satisfactorily in 1992 (Onumah, 1995).

In 1991 the Garu Bank, a small rural bank set up in 1983 in Ghana, was near to collapse as a result of embezzlement and bad loans. The people of Garu persuaded a member of their own community who was working in Accra to come back to the area and become the man-ager. The Bank is a unit bank and operates relatively autonomously. Share capital of the Bank is owned by the local community, the Catholic Mission, the local Agricultural Station and a Disabled Rehabilitation Centre. Helped by an additional capital injection of $30,000 received from overseas donors via the Catholic Mission the manager trans-formed the situation, and expected to report a profit for the first time.

The bank has a range of clients, including local salaried workers such as teachers and government employees. These people are good customers because they take loans which are easily recoverable in the form of deductions made from their salaries at source.

Alongside these customers, the Bank provides services to some 300 farmers' groups. Some of these groups were originally formed by the local Agricultural Station and the Catholic Mission and bought shares in the Bank when it was first set up. The manager went to meet the groups to discuss their needs with them. He has developed his own approach to the groups, and stresses that they should be concerned with working together rather than just obtaining credit. He has set up his own criteria for lending to the groups: savings balances of at least 10 per cent of the loan amount; regularity of savings as an indicator of group cohesion; and that the group should have been operating for at least six months. Repayment of the loan on time results in almost automatic qualification for a new loan the following year (although he had refused loans to a number of groups the previous year due to poor performance). (Source: Abugre, Johnson *et al*, 1995.)

This bank manager may be exceptional. However, NGOs could provide an important bridge between these banks and savings groups and help to negotiate facilities and services for the groups by, for example, helping to gain access to funds which are used as a line of credit by the bank itself to such groups. In some cases as in the example below, such business turns out to be more profitable than the bank's existing portfolio!

In Northern Bangladesh, the International Fund for Agricultural Development has since 1989 been financing the German Technical Assistance Agency, GTZ, to bring an NGO (RDRS: Rangpur Dinajpur Rural Services) into partnership with four banks including a government owned one (RAKUB). The NGO promotes and trains groups to the point where the groups go to the banks for loans. The banks bear all the lending risk. So far some 1,800 groups, of 10 to 20 members, have been trained. Repayment is good, and has probably been influenced by the ethos of the Grameen Bank and its imitators, so numerous in rural Bangladesh. The banks claim they are making a profit (of something like six per cent on each taka loaned) whereas they make a loss on most of their normal business. About US$1.8 million had been lent up to mid-1995. (Source: Chauduri, 1994.)

A further example is a formal-sector bank in Sri Lanka, which has developed a concept of 'barefoot banking'. Its staff take their services to people in their homes, and the bank works with NGOs to make links to groups of micro-entrepreneurs, relying on NGOs to address the social needs of the entrepreneurs (Wijesundera, 1996).

2.8.4 Linking with specialised financial service NGOs

If an NGO decides that direct provision of financial services is the best way forward, it may still not be necessary for that NGO to provide the services. A number of NGOs, local and international, have developed skills and experience in financial service provision and may be interested in starting work in a new area. It may prove more effective for these specialised NGOs to manage such an intervention separately from the existing NGO's activities.

2.8.5 Advocacy

Another strategy for NGOs experienced in advocacy may be to persuade banks to extend financial services to hitherto unserved areas and to poor people in general (WWB, 1994).

2.9 Summary and conclusions

While the overview of informal financial services given here has been brief, there is ample evidence to demonstrate that there is usually a range of such services in existence which poor people are already using. This is the background against which any plan to provide financial services should be considered.

Exploring the array of existing informal services available to different groups in an area can provide a wealth of information. Talking to users and assessing how existing financial intermediation interacts with other local markets and social and economic structures can help to establish the degree to which it is enabling or exploitative, and for whom. Where an NGO is considering intervention, an understanding of existing informal services may provide useful indicators for design, in terms of size, timing, and volume of savings and loans.

However it cannot be assumed that NGOs should intervene directly. Indeed, experience suggests that NGOs may lack the ability to manage funds (rather than simply channel them). NGOs may inadvertently damage existing satisfactory financial services by charging interest rates that are too low (and therefore artificially divert demand) or may create indebtedness.

There are alternatives to direct provision by NGOs which might involve promotion of services rather than provision. For example, an NGO might make use of its strengths in community mobilisation and training to link up with existing or potential suppliers of financial services in more sustainable ways.

- The NGO should investigate the nature and characteristics of financial services already available in order to establish how, for whom, and under what circumstances these services enable or exploit the livelihoods of poor people; understand the services which people value and how they use them, in order to avoid undermining those aspects they find beneficial and would wish to retain; collect information on loan and deposit sizes, types, terms and conditions, which can contribute to the design of new services; and, where poverty reduction is the aim, relate proposals to an analysis of how poverty would be reduced by the intervention.

- The NGO should carefully consider whether its staff have the appropriate skills and experience to provide financial services before embarking on a path of direct provision.

- The NGO should consider alternatives to direct provision of financial services and explore the range of options that might exist, such as building relations with banks, developing internal credit facilities within groups, or linking groups to the formal sector.

3

The design of savings and credit schemes for poor people

3.1 Introduction

In the preceding chapter, the role of informal financial services, and how this can be taken into account when deciding whether and how to intervene, has been discussed. This chapter and the two subsequent ones discuss the design, performance, sustainability, and impact of interventions to provide financial services.

In the recent past, the best-known microfinance institutions (such as Grameen Bank, Bangladesh, Bank Rakyat Indonesia, and Banco Sol, Bolivia) have achieved high repayment rates, yet most of the people who use them would not have been able to make use of the financial services provided by the formal sector. The design of such schemes has increasingly involved the use of innovative forms of loan collateral, and higher interest rates on loans. Little attention has been given to monitoring the uses to which loans are put, and much more attention has been paid to savings, including their use as a form of collateral. Table 3.1 summarises the rationale behind some of these design features, which are discussed in more detail below. However, a particular combination of design features will have different outcomes under different circumstances. As a result implementors need to look critically at this combination in understanding the results they see in practice.

3.2 Targeting savings and credit to poor people

A major concern of NGOs involved in credit provision has always been how to reach poor people, and in the late 1980s and 1990s the rhetoric that NGOs are able 'to reach the poorest' has remained powerful. Some organisations target the poor by defining the criteria which users have to meet in order to be eligible for loans; but 'self-targeting' is increasingly becoming a feature of the design

Table 3.1 Design features for ensuring high repayment rates on loans and enabling poor people to access credit

Design Feature	Intended Effect
1	
Access methods	(Means of ensuring that relatively well-off people do not crowd out others' access to loans)
Maximum income/assets	Direct exclusion of better-off through eg land-holding ceiling
Small loan size	Loans are small enough that better-off are not interested in them
Regular meetings	Indirect exclusion of better-off through eg compulsory attendance at weekly meetings or contributions of physical labour to which the wealthy will not agree
2	
Screening techniques	(Mechanisms for screening out bad borrowers and projects)
Market interest rates	Encourages loan taking on basis of prospective returns not to capture subsidies
Self-selected	Prospective members are asked to form groups themselves and hence screen in favour of those they believe will repay, they also screen proposed loan use
Character reference	Alternatively local officials or power structures may be used to approve loan applications
3	
Incentives to repay	(Mechanisms for giving borrowers who have no collateral incentives to repay, or failing this, forcing them to repay)
Intensive supervision	Regular meetings with extension staff in or near the homes of borrowers
Peer group monitoring	Repayment is made in public in front of the group with consequent loss of face if payment is not made
Borrower incentives	For example, rebates of interest on loans repaid early
Agency staff incentives	Agency staff may receive financial bonuses directly related to the repayment performance of their clients
Progressive lending	Borrowers are able to gain repeated access to loans if they repay and these may also increase in size
Compulsory Savings	A small amount contributed regularly into a group savings fund provides insurance or collateral for the loans of all group members

(Source: Adapted from Hulme and Mosley, 1996.)

of interventions, with members choosing to join the scheme as a result of the services on offer rather than the implementors of the scheme choosing them.

NGOs have often implemented a first stage of targeting when they decide the geographical area in which to work, since they may have selected this on the basis of a range of poverty indicators. But geographical targeting alone may be imprecise. There are degrees of poverty in all communities. The next step may be to exclude those with whom the NGO does not wish to work. This can be done in various ways, for example, by defining an asset or land-holding ceiling for members; many of the well-known schemes in Bangladesh impose a land-holding ceiling of half an acre. However, while it may act as a guide when field staff are recruiting new members, Rutherford (1995b) points out that NGO workers do not usually seek proof of the size of land-holding, and it is easy to disguise or conceal the amount held; as a result the rule is not strictly enforced.

In a number of ACTIONAID programmes, direct exclusion is practised through the use of wealth-ranking exercises (see Pretty *et al,* 1995). On the basis of the results, project staff identify those in the lower part of the ranking whom it wishes to target; staff may approach these individuals directly to form groups as a basis for a range of development activities, including savings and credit.

An alternative to directly targeting a particular group is to use design features which result in the better-off excluding themselves. Two such design features have been used by many schemes: small loan sizes and the holding of compulsory regular meetings to qualify for loans and to make repayments. Richer people are less likely to be interested in very small loans or in attending regular meetings, whereas repayment at weekly or fortnightly meetings may be attractive to poorer people who feel able to manage small, regular cash repayments out of their normal income.

In practice, schemes often combine several methods of targeting. For example, having initially selected a relatively poor area to work in, the design of the scheme may include maximum loan sizes and regular meetings with a group who may have been selected using wealth-ranking techniques.

Some organisations have assessed the proportion of 'non-target' households in their membership. Figures from BRAC's 1995 impact study (Mustafa *et al,* 1996) indicate that 10 per cent of members were from 'non-target' households. Targeting is rarely an exact science and can be a time-consuming, and therefore costly, activity. Indirect mechanisms which promote 'self-selection' are able to lower these costs. However, as the scale of operations increases, so these mechanisms are less easy to monitor and there is likely to be an increase in the proportion of non-target households involved. Some organisations regard this as an inevitable but acceptable trade-off.

3.3 Women as users of financial services

Making women the beneficiaries of NGO credit schemes is also a targeting technique. Women — whether poor or not — suffer discrimination in the market (Kabeer, 1996). It is thus important to ensure that women can obtain loans provided by intervention agencies.

It was pointed out in Chapter 1 that women can be targeted for reasons of efficiency in implementation rather than because of a concern for women's empowerment. This emphasises the need for clarity as to the reason for targeting women, the means of doing it, and the likely outcome in terms of gender relations. Microfinance interventions may lead to empowerment for women by increasing their incomes and their control over that income, enhancing their knowledge and skills in production and trade, and increasing their participation in household decision-making. As a result, social attitudes and perceptions may change, and women's status in the household and community may be enhanced.

A useful distinction to be made is between *receiving* a loan and *using* it. The investigation carried out in Bangladesh by Goetz and Sen Gupta, demonstrated that, even when it was women who received the loans, gender relations within the household affected how loans were used, and the degree of control the woman borrower retained over their use. It is therefore important to understand what happens to a loan beyond its disbursement to a female borrower.

In addition, attendance at regular meetings can involve a heavy cost in terms of time for women, especially for poorer women, who in many socio-economic environments have heavier workloads than better-off women or men. There may, on the other hand, be circumstances in which the group approach and regular meetings have empowering outcomes for women (Hashemi *et al*, 1996; Osmani, 1996). One rationale for using groups is that where programmes are intended to reach women, group-based activities mean that women are able to defend their attendance as a social role and obligation. In addition, where women are socially isolated, for example as a result of purdah restrictions on their mobility, meeting other women at the home of a friend or neighbour may be of intrinsic value. The role of the group meeting is thus likely to vary in different social contexts; women borrowers themselves should be involved in determining the role and organisation of group meetings.

3.4 Lending through groups

The well-known microfinance schemes in Bangladesh, such as those of BRAC and the Grameen Bank, tend to work through groups. Indeed, such schemes are often referred to as 'group-based finance' or 'solidarity-group lending' schemes. Because group members are jointly liable for each individual's loans, this represents a form of 'social collateral'. This contrasts to the physical collateral of land or assets which formal-sector services usually require and which poor people are unable to offer. The rationale of group-based lending is that if a member is having difficulty with repayments, others in the group will put pressure on that member to repay. Further, that if this pressure fails and the member defaults on the loan, the whole group will repay the loan on behalf of the member.

Despite the popularity of group-based lending as a design feature, the function which groups play in the scheme can vary: as we have seen, women may find meetings time-wasting, or an important social event, depending on their circumstances. Recent research into the way in which group solidarity operates in practice is illuminating in this respect. First, it is worth clarifying what is meant by 'groups'. Some microfinance schemes have small groups of five or six members, called 'solidarity groups'. A number of these small groups may then come together as 'development centres' or village organisations. Alternatively, a group of some 20 or so people may operate without sub-groups. Weekly meetings for saving and loan repayment are usually organised at the level of the larger group. Staff of the scheme are thus able to meet more clients at one time and hence reduce the costs of providing the service. The ratio of costs to loan size is very high when loans are for small amounts.

Of course, NGOs often have other motives for working with groups: they use them to implement other activities, such as literacy classes and health education; they may also see them as a means for further organisation-building in the area.

3.4.1 Functions of the group in microfinance schemes

The role which groups play in the operation of microfinance schemes can be analysed as follows:

Targeting: regular compulsory group meetings may serve to discourage better-off people from taking part, increasing the funds available for lending to poor people.

Transparency: the openness and accountability which meetings can bring to the process of taking and repaying credit can also prevent certain members of the group colluding with field workers or bank staff over the allocation of credit.

Screening of potential borrowers: where groups are formed through self-selection, the individual members effectively screen each other, initially selecting those of their neighbours and friends whom they believe to be capable of repaying the loans. This is especially true in the case of small 'solidarity groups'.

Incentives to repay: if repayments are made at group meetings it is immediately obvious to everyone involved if someone is falling behind with their repayments. Social pressure may then be exerted on these members to repay by other members and by staff of the scheme. Viewed negatively this is a form of public humiliation for those who start to fall behind with repayments. The social pressure is then expected to act as an incentive to them to either work harder or obtain the repayments from another source.

Enforcing repayment: the group as a whole may be penalised by being refused further loans if a member defaults or falls behind with repayments. The policy may then be that the group's savings balances will be used to repay the loan if necessary.

Two recent studies have looked at what happens in practice when members fall behind with repayments. Jain (1996) reports that, in the case of Grameen Bank, the concept of joint responsibility was much discussed, but when members fell behind with repayments they were in fact followed up on an individual basis by bank staff in household visits. Moreover, other group members were not penalised by having to make payments on behalf of defaulting members or through forfeiting further loans. Jain goes on to point out that the functioning of the Grameen Bank's development centres as autonomous groups is relatively limited. The leaders of the group have a minor role in credit management and it tends to be Bank staff who actually develop relationships with group members. Jain judges the importance of group meetings to lie in the fact that all transactions are open and staff are thus accountable to group members. This has the important effect of limiting the ability of staff to undermine the system by favouring particular individuals or using their position to further their own objectives. The routine of regular meetings also serves to enforce repayment discipline.

In the case of BRAC, it was found that in the early stages of a borrower finding difficulty with repayment, she would first approach relatives and close friends for assistance (Montgomery, 1996). If the situation continued, it was the village-level group that was approached by the BRAC fieldworker rather than the five or six-member solidarity group. The most forceful sanction was the withdrawal of further loans from the larger village group as a whole, and it appears that the effect of this sanction was for the defaulting member to drop out of the scheme. The evidence from BRAC also demonstrates that, while groups can be a source of social pressure on borrowing members to repay, it does not appear to be the case that group members always pay for an individual borrower's loans in the event of default.

3.4.2 Including the poorest

A major concern in connection with the use of self-selecting solidarity groups for financial service provision is that, given the way in which members screen each other, it is the poorest who are least likely to be able to join the scheme. This concern appears to be supported by Montgomery's research on BRAC which showed that those who dropped out after repayment difficulties tended to be the poorer members. However, by contrast SANASA in Sri Lanka demonstrates how people with different levels of relative wealth can be included by operating a range of financial services which respond to the circumstances which poorer households face:

SANASA has a three-tier structure of primary societies, district unions, and a national federation which accommodates 8,000 village-level thrift and credit co-operatives with 800,000 members. Village-level groups are highly heterogeneous and vary in size from 20 to 700 members, with the larger ones having turned themselves into small-scale banks. The second and third tiers of this pyramidal structure provide financial and technical support to the village-level co-operatives. SANASA has a strong ideology of self-reliance, savings mobilisation, and the profitable provision of financial services to its members. In practice the upper levels of the structure are strongly dependent on donor funds.

Village-level co-operatives have an open and participatory structure with monthly meetings of the general membership, and are run by a small elected management committee. The financial statements of the co-operative and member's business are discussed at the monthly meetings. Financial information is in some cases also written on the wall of the book-keeping room. Such transparency at meetings reduces the likelihood of malpractice and take-over by elites, which has caused failure of co-operatives in Sri Lanka in the past.

The financial services offered by the co-operatives are varied and flexible. A village group is autonomous and decides its own range of loan types and savings facilities, which evolve in relation to members' needs and local economic circumstances. A society of 60 members may have as many as ten different types of credit facility.

SANASA has attempted to convince primary societies of the viability of bringing poorer members into the co-operatives, and providing services which will meet their needs. One way of making it possible for poor people to join is to allow the member's share to be purchased in monthly instalments rather than as a single payment.

Of particular interest to poorer members are 'instant loans', and facilities with interest rates varying according to type of access and length of deposit.

Instant loans, even at high interest-rates but with overnight access, enable those facing a crisis to respond to it without further endangering their livelihoods. Such facilities act as protection mechanisms reducing the vulnerability of households to shocks and enhancing their coping strategies.

Data from SANASA shows that poorer people tend to take smaller loans, because they do not wish to expose themselves to the additional risks that a debt burden represents.

SANASA has come to understand the importance of 'hot' money. This is money generated from savings and member's shares, and default on loans from these funds constitutes 'stealing' from other members. This is a further factor for enhancing peer pressure, and shows the importance of limiting the amount of 'cold' money (i.e. funds supplied by banks and external donors) in the system, which may encourage members not to repay.

(Sources: Montgomery, 1996; Hulme and Montgomery, 1994.)

3.4.3 Other examples of group-based schemes

The dynamics of groups, once in place, need to be carefully observed to ensure that the results are as intended. The case studies examined in Chapter 6 further demonstrate the different ways in which the group concept can be employed in practice. In three cases the groups involve more or less everyone in the locality and are therefore very large, upwards of 30-40 people and sometimes as many as 100. The sanction of refusing new loans if there is non-payment is the main mechanism used to enforce repayment. In two of the schemes studied, Casa Campesina Cayambe (CCC) and ACTIONAID in the Gambia, groups are closely related to local institutional structures, which can present dilemmas for implementors. Groups of this nature tend to cut across socio-economic divisions and there is the potential for relatively better-off members to abuse the scheme by ensuring that they themselves get loans. They might also justify not allocating loans to poorer members by arguing that they are not creditworthy and will not repay.

The use of joint liability and social collateral mechanisms can improve repayment performance. There are other ways of building a sense of identity with the scheme and encouraging reliable repayment. Participation in the operation and decision-making structures of the scheme is likely to promote a sense of ownership on the part of users. In three of the case studies in Chapter 6, URAC, Ladywood Credit Union, and CCC, members are involved in committees which review performance, allocate new credit, and advise on policies and practice.

Repayment is likely to be enhanced by the use of 'hot' rather than 'cold' money, as explained in the account of SANASA above. There is supporting evidence for this from India in the case of MYRADA, Community Development Fund, and ASSEFA (Bennett, Goldberg and Hunte, 1996, Copestake, 1996a). Members' sense of ownership of the scheme is less when loan funds are from external sources than when they are from members' savings. This has been compounded by the prevalence of cheap externally-provided credit in the past, coupled with a lack of concern about repayment.

While many schemes use groups, Hulme and Mosley concluded from their study of 12 microfinance institutions (1996) that groups are not always a crucial feature of scheme design. There are examples of institutions success-fully providing financial services to poor people by dealing directly with individuals. Bank Rakyat Indonesia (BRI) (see Chapter 1) and BAAC in Thailand are two such examples. BRI makes use of the local knowledge of village-based agents in deciding whether to approve loans to new borrowers. The case study of Ladywood Credit Union in Chapter 6 provides another example of lending on an individual basis; in fact, credit union legislation in the UK stipulates that the privacy of the individual must be preserved.

3.5 Savings

Poor people hold savings in many forms, including assets such as animals, grain or jewellery. The account of informal services presented in Chapter 2 demonstrates that, given the opportunity, people will save in cash. In discussing the design of a savings component, the purposes for which people save, and the characteristics that savings services need to have in order to meet their requirements, must first be clarified.

Saving in the form of assets has limitations. Grain can deteriorate in storage or be lost to pests; animals require looking after and can die; moreover, when they are held as insurance against crises such as drought, they are often sold at a loss if the crisis occurs, because of deteriorating terms of trade or the need for a quick sale. Holding a visible and available form of savings, such as grain or assets, can make it hard to resist demands and claims from other relatives. Jewellery is relatively illiquid as an asset unless it can easily be pawned at times of need. When people save in cash, they often keep it in their homes, where it is at risk of theft and loss in case of fire. Small amounts of accessible cash are always needed for emergencies, ranging in scope from unexpected guests to death or illness in the family.

The purposes of saving can be summarised as follows:

- **daily financial management:** the need to keep cash safely in order to manage and deal with day-to-day expenses and occurrences, including emergencies;

- **consumption smoothing:** dealing with seasonality or unemployment by holding over income from one time period to another;

- **accumulation:** building up savings balances in order to undertake future large expenditures, such as the purchase of housing materials or agricultural implements, or payment of school fees;

- **insurance:** building up savings balances to deal with irregular events such as illness, marriages, and funerals.

3.5.1 The value of a savings facility

People are well aware of the risks involved in saving and as a result value safe places to keep their cash. They may look for a range of attributes in a savings facility, including:

- **safety:** will their savings be held safely by the bank or other depositor?

- **ease of withdrawal:** can they get quick access to their money when they need it?

- **proximity** to home or workplace: ease of access in terms of distance and time;

- **prizes or bonuses** for good saving;

- **high interest rates:** worthwhile monetary return on saving;

- **informality of procedures** and polite treatment when making deposits or withdrawals.

The above list is the result of a ranking exercise undertaken with BRI customers (BRI, no date). It is notable that safety and ease of access come very near the top of this list and that monetary returns in the form of interest rates and prizes are lower priorities. It is also likely that women and men will rank these attributes differently, since they may have different purposes in saving.

Until recently, savings services have been a relatively neglected component of microfinance debate and practice. Definitions of poverty based on the inadequacy of income focus on the shortage of capital available for investment, and many financial interventions attempt to alleviate this constraint by using external funds to make capital available. However, studies of informal financial services (see Chapter 2) show that poor people value a savings facility as a contribution to economic security. For NGOs and other donors, part of the emphasis on credit may have resulted from the fact that delivery of credit utilises donor funds whereas mobilising savings does not.

3.5.2 Compulsory or voluntary savings?

A distinction is often made between 'compulsory' and 'voluntary' savings. In a compulsory system, saving is either required as a condition of membership or in order to receive loans. In contrast, voluntary savings schemes allow members to make deposits whenever they wish.

Compulsory and voluntary savings are characteristic of two fundamentally different philosophies (Robinson, 1995). Compulsory savings schemes 'assume that the poor must be taught to save, and that they need to learn financial discipline. [Voluntary savings schemes] assume that the working poor already save, and that what is needed are institutions and services appropriate for their needs.'(p.6) It appears that people always need savings accounts but that loans are needed only occasionally. The fact that BRI has 14.5 million deposit accounts and only 2.3 million loan accounts supports such an argument.

When compulsory savings schemes are tied to borrowing, very poor people may decide not to participate, because they are reluctant to take on debts; or they may be excluded by existing members who fear such people will be unable to repay the loans out of regular income. Rutherford (1995a) argues that savings facilities that are flexible and voluntary, and which allow people to build savings balances independently of debt, are an unmet demand of poor people in many of these schemes. It is this kind of service which can effectively reduce poverty by enabling people to protect their incomes.

There is now, therefore, growing appreciation of the demand for flexible savings facilities for poor people. Saving small amounts regularly, and feeling a sense of obligation to do this, are positive features for many people, for whom the discipline involved is important. This realisation is resulting in new designs for savings accounts. Buro Tangail, for example, a financial services NGO in Bangladesh, is introducing a range of accounts allowing users to choose one which meets their needs. These include a fully flexible savings account, and accounts which involve a fixed weekly deposit over a number of years.

Drawing on the successful experience of BRI in mobilising savings, Robinson has suggested some of the conditions which need to be in place in order to launch voluntary savings services. The first of these is an enabling macro-economic environment, with relatively low and stable levels of inflation, and an appropriate legal and regulatory environment, together with political stability and suitable demographic conditions. As she points out 'Beginning savings mobilization in the midst of hyperinflation, civil war or in a sparsely populated desert are not recommended!' (1995, p.2). However, few economic environments are as 'enabling' as Robinson would like. Indeed, in this context the meaning of the word is unclear (Yaqub, 1996). Moreover, the work of URAC in Mexico (one of the case studies) shows that voluntary savings schemes can work well even in the presence of high inflation.

The second condition concerns government supervision arrangements for institutions taking deposits. In order to protect users, deposit-taking institutions must be regulated. Existing legislation in many countries is a constraint on NGOs' mobilising savings and taking deposits themselves. Organisations which are not formally registered as banks may face restrictions on their ability to take deposits. If the NGO facilitates the opening of savings accounts in local banks on behalf of its depositors, it cannot use funds from this source for on-lending to other members. There are good reasons for such regulations; NGOs are not necessarily suitable institutions to hold deposits.

Third, Robinson stresses the history, capability, and performance of the institution. She emphasises the responsibility that taking savings entails (it is easier to learn to manage your own funds through credit first) and the complexity of operating a savings scheme properly.

3.5.3 Linking savings to credit

Whether savings are compulsory or voluntary, there is often a link between the savings component and access to credit. The link can be formed in a variety of ways:

- The amount of the loan may be a fixed multiple of the amount deposited (savings flow) over a given period. By making savings deposits of a certain level, the client demonstrates his or her ability to repay a loan with similar repayments out of regular income.

- The amount of the loan may be a fixed multiple of the amount saved (savings stock).

- Once a loan has been taken, the savings in the account may be retained as collateral for the loan, and withdrawals taking the balance below a certain level not permitted.

In these ways savings can act as part of the lender's screening process. By observing the savings behaviour of borrowers, the lender can judge whether borrowers are good risks, and their capacity to manage debt. This also helps to prevent the lender indebting a borrower by being over-optimistic about the borrower's ability to repay.

The case studies in Chapter 6 illustrate the way in which these mechanisms have been applied in practice. In the case of SUNGI in Pakistan, compulsory minimum monthly savings are a criterion for receiving a loan, although the loan amount is assessed in relation to the purpose proposed. In Mexico, URAC operates a system by which an applicant for a loan must be making regular savings with the scheme, and the maximum loan amount is five times the savings balance. In the case of Ladywood Credit Union in the UK, loan size is a maximum of twice the savings balance, and the repayment plan is drawn up in discussion with the borrower and in relation to their savings record. In this way the scheme attempts to set instalment levels just below the amounts previously deposited in order to ensure that the savings balance continues to rise so that the borrower's financial security is not being eroded by taking the loan.

3.6 Forms of loan

Some microfinance institutions make loans in kind as well as in cash; many require applicants to specify what they are going to use the loan for, with cash credit being 'directed' to particular uses, because lenders often prefer loans to be used for production rather than consumption. This sub-section considers the advantages and disadvantages of loans 'in kind' and directed credit. (Loans which are both given in kind and repaid in kind are not discussed here; see Fall (1991), Strachan and Peters (forthcoming) for accounts of cereal banks and similar schemes.)

3.6.1 Credit in cash or kind?

Credit is sometimes provided 'in kind' by schemes, in the form of seeds, tools, fertilisers, larger agricultural tools such as ploughs and weeders, or as inputs for construction and home improvement. The main arguments given for such provision usually relate to the local unavailability of the goods supplied. The NGO may supply the goods directly or provide vouchers for redemption against specified items in particular retail outlets. Of our case studies, URAC provides vouchers for the purchase of building material through local suppliers under the terms of its construction loans.

Direct supply by an NGO lender can lead to a range of problems:

- It makes the borrower dependent on the NGO for inputs and the NGO will tend to be blamed if the tool or other input is in some way faulty or does not arrive on time.

- It can prevent the development of a local market for the inputs if they are supplied from outside the area, making it unviable for suppliers to set up locally. An alternative is for the NGO to ensure that inputs are obtained from local suppliers.

- The NGO is likely to incur large costs which are not usually included in the amount of the loan. In effect borrowers receive an additional grant in the form of transport costs, and they may not be able to afford to pay these costs when the NGO stops supplying.

Most NGOs prefer to issue loans in cash rather than kind. The borrower is then able to use the credit as he or she sees fit and to purchase any materials required. The borrower then takes full responsibility for the result so cannot allege sub-standard and inappropriate inputs as an excuse for not repaying the loan. Furthermore, the costs of transporting cash tend to be lower than those of transporting seed, fertiliser or machinery, thus reducing the operating costs of the NGO. Local suppliers are likely to respond to the local demand generated and this in the longer run will reduce transport costs for everyone. Nevertheless, if the lending institution has proven integrity in supplying goods of high quality, it may work to the advantage of the borrower. An example in the case of URAC is the vet who provides animals instead of cash loans and with them a short-term guarantee of the animal's health.

3.6.2 Directed or undirected credit?

In schemes where cash loans are given, credit may be 'directed' to certain purposes. It is often specified that loans should be for productive purposes, because lenders fear that if the loan were used for other purposes it would be less likely to be repaid. It is assumed that repayments need to come out of *additional* income, accruing from productive investment.

An alternative view is that the household economy has a range of production and consumption activities which are related in complex ways, so that a distinction between them is artificial. The borrower should be allowed to make use of the cash credit as she or he sees fit. Attempting to direct the credit to a particular purpose is inefficient, because it is very difficult for the lender to monitor the exact use to which loans are put. If loans are specified as being for productive purposes only, the household may state such a purpose in the loan application but may not use the money in this way in practice. Evidence suggests that loans are likely to be split up and used to cover a range of household needs and expenditure. Therefore the lender should not be concerned with what the loan is used for as long as it is repaid.

Demonstration of the interconnectedness of consumption and production activities can be illustrated using the case of pre-harvest loans in seasonal agriculture. In land-abundant areas, loans to make food for consumption available at this time can also be viewed as production loans, as they might enable farmers to continue to work on their fields and hence represent an investment in productive capacity. Farmers may no longer need to spend time undertaking casual labour on other people's farms to earn money to buy food; or loans may simply ensure that nutritional requirements are met so that farmers are able to carry out work on their own farm.

Clearly these arguments do not necessarily apply where a scheme is lending to micro- or small-scale enterprises. Loans for such purposes tend to be larger in size and usually involve a more direct relationship between the lender and borrower. In the course of this relationship it is likely that the lender will undertake an appraisal of the investment with the borrower before approving the loan. (This is not an area examined in detail in this book; see Barrow and Barrow, 1992.)

However, once undirected cash loans are in place, loan facilities directed to specific purposes have a role. In two of the case studies, URAC and Casa Campesina Cayambe (CCC), there are a range of loan facilities available. The 'normal' cash loans can be used for any purpose and carry no restrictions. But larger loans are available for specific purposes, such as house-building, constructing bathrooms, or for productive enterprises. The advantage of such directed loans are that the repayment schedules can be tailored to suit the type of investment being made. Housing loans, for example, tend to have longer repayment terms than other loans.

Schemes which offer emergency loans are usually concerned to protect their members from the potentially impoverishing effects of events such as illness or death in the family. A loan which is easily available at short notice in response to such events might prevent the borrower having to sell valued assets such as livestock or jewellery. Of the case studies, CCC has this kind of loan facility, which provides special credit in the case of illness or domestic emergency. Loan approval in such cases by-passes the usual process but requires a doctor's certificate in the case of illness or endorsement by a member of the Community Committee in the case of other domestic emergencies. Similar procedures to enable quick disbursement of loans in emergencies are also available to members of URAC and Ladywood Credit Union.

3.7 Loan disbursement and repayment schedules

The model of loan scheme that has become dominant in Bangladesh involves members holding loans on a more or less continuous basis. For example, in the Association for Social Advancement, disbursement follows a very strict schedule: once the member has saved for a certain number of weeks, usually 12, she or he is eligible for a loan which is repaid in fixed amounts over the following 50 weeks. As soon as this loan is repaid the borrower becomes eligible for another one. While this system can be seen as helpful in terms of its simple and mechanical rules, it has been criticised for its lack of flexibility; members take on loans when they are available rather than when the borrowers want them. It is a system which requires people to go into debt in order to make use of their capacity to save: the loan is a lump sum to be received now and repaid by saving over the next 50 weeks.

Such a system can force people to adopt complicated strategies to manage the funds until they actually need them, if they do not wish to miss their turn to obtain a loan. This helps to explain the myriad of on-lending arrangements that usually exist between group members (Rutherford, 1995a).

This problem is not encountered in systems where members can take loans at times appropriate to them. The case study scheme in Pakistan, run by SUNGI, which is most closely modelled on the Bangladesh schemes, also operates a system of loan applications to be made via the village organisations' credit committees, but there is no pressure to take a loan once a member is eligible. Flexibility in amounts and timing of disbursement seem to be significant factors in providing a credit mechanism which poor people can manage in relation to their livelihood strategies.

An approach based on small cash-loans with simple and easily verifiable criteria, such as attendance at meetings, and appropriate savings deposits or balances, enables greater decentralisation in decision-making over loan applications. This, in turn, means that the lead time between application and disbursement is likely to be reduced, which is more convenient to the borrower.

The timeliness of loan disbursement is crucial when loans are being used for seasonal activities such as agriculture. If a programme of seasonal loans is in place which farmers utilise to buy inputs or prepare land then complicated appraisal and approval procedures which might delay disbursement are unhelpful. Farmers will not be able to undertake farming activities when they would wish to, and the usefulness of the credit to them is much reduced. This can in turn worsen the prospects of repayment if they are highly dependent on agriculture for income.

Repayment schedules involving small and frequent instalments are one of the principal features of the 'new' design of credit. As mentioned above, it has been demonstrated that in a variety of circumstances, borrowers are able to repay loans out of regular income and need not rely on the income generated from a specific and identifiable investment. In the past, repayment schedules linked to income streams on investments have often been over-optimistic in their expectations and hence borrowers have not been able to keep up repayments. Loans for micro-enterprises are rather different in nature, but 'little and often' may also be a good rule of thumb for loan repayment instalments in these cases.

However, in some areas where seasonality is a highly significant factor and cash is virtually unavailable at certain times of year, there is also a need for flexibility in repayment schedules. In these circumstances, lower levels of repayment could be arranged during particularly difficult months and higher ones at times when market activity and incomes revive. Even here, the principle of repayment of loans out of regular income can be retained.

3.8 Interest rates

Interest rates are an issue over which there has been much debate among microfinance practitioners (see Chapter 1). Along with the diagnosis of the problem as a shortage of investment capital available to poor households goes the assumption that credit obtainable from local informal sources carries too high an interest rate. Before continuing this discussion it is important to understand what an interest rate is.

Put simply, the interest rate is the price of money. As a price it is made up of a number of components as far as the lender is concerned. It is the means through which the lender:

- pays for the cost of the funds that are being lent (cost of capital); if these are from savers then the savers are likely to expect a return which will at least cover inflation and so maintain the value of their savings;

- recovers the costs of providing the service (costs of administration): the costs of the staff employed to give and recover loans, and the costs of the offices, vehicles and stationery that are necessary to provide that service;

- covers losses as a result of those who default on their loans (costs of default).

The interest rate which is charged to borrowers is usually called the 'nominal' interest rate. This may be different from the 'real' interest rate, which is roughly calculated as the nominal interest rate minus the rate of inflation in the country (this approximation works best at low rates of inflation). The rate of inflation indicates the degree to which money is declining in value over time. If the nominal interest rate is higher than the rate of inflation, then the real interest rate is positive. For borrowers, a positive real interest rate means that they have actually paid something for the benefit of using the money that they have borrowed; and for savers, that the money they receive back will buy more than their original deposit would have done.

In recent years many NGOs have accepted the need to charge interest rates which cover inflation and make a contribution to costs. This means interest rates which are positive in real terms and comparable to those charged by formal-sector banks (sometimes termed 'market' interest rates). As discussed in Chapter 1, this differs from earlier practice when the provision of credit by NGOs and state banks was usually at subsidised rates. This 'cheap' credit was attractive to borrowers outside the target group, and was diverted away from its intended purposes; and loans were often not repaid. This combination of 'cheap' credit and widespread default resulted in the rapid erosion of loan funds.

The importance of charging a rate of interest which covers the costs of inflation, administration, and default is that the loan fund is able to revolve and maintain its value. In the past, revolving funds have often dwindled as a result of these costs. Where the loan fund is generated out of members' savings rather than given as a grant by donors, it is even more essential to ensure that its value is maintained.

However, the ability to cover all of the administrative costs through the interest charged to borrowers is only likely to develop over a period of time, as the system of lending becomes more efficient and a greater number of borrowers are receiving loans. Attempting to recover costs in the early stages of a scheme is likely to result in interest rates which are excessively high.

When comparing interest rates with those of formal-sector banks it is also important to recognise the hidden costs that poor borrowers face when they approach banks. They may be charged loan fees, have to organise 'gifts' for bank staff, and incur transport costs to get there. Worse, they may be treated with disdain and even contempt — not a monetary cost, but a cost all the same. The actual price that the borrower is paying for loans from these sources is therefore higher than the interest rate alone; and the attitude of bank staff can make the transaction even more burdensome. This is why loans which carry interest rates comparable to the formal sector are still likely to be positively regarded by clients.

3.9 Integrating financial services with other activities

Few NGOs provide savings and credit services without getting involved in related development activities. For ACTIONAID and Oxfam an integrated approach is usually seen as essential in addressing the causes of poverty identified in a particular area or by a particular group of people; it is rarely the case that savings and credit activities alone will reduce poverty. A range of other constraints are likely to exist, especially in making use of credit for production purposes. For example, numeracy may be a need for women who want to embark on petty trading and keep records to find out if they are actually making money; preventive health programmes may be the best way to reduce the need for credit to meet health-care expenses.

NGOs may have a number of objectives in integrating savings and credit into their other activities, and a range of ways of doing so. Here we will distinguish between three approaches: first, where the NGO's objective is to form groups which will function as social organisations in their own right rather than being solely for the purposes of providing credit; second, where groups are an effective means of delivering related development activities, such as literacy and health education; third, where savings and credit activities overlap with other services, such as business and skills training, to promote economic activities.

An integrated approach does not necessarily mean that staff are involved in delivering all aspects of the programme and are therefore generalists. Interventions may be operationally distinct, involving several specialist staff. We have argued for the need for strong staff skills in Chapter 2, and will suggest in Chapter 4 the benefits of keeping programme accounts entirely separate.

3.9.1 Savings and credit for group formation and institution-building

In some cases, forming groups is not simply a means of delivering savings and credit services but of building up group skills as part of a wider strategy of 'empowerment'. An analysis of poverty which holds that powerlessness rather than low income is the main problem may lead to the view that collective action has an important role in bringing about change. The NGO is likely to work with the group to enable it to develop its own analysis of the situation, and plan and implement solutions to problems, which might range from building a water supply to campaigning for land rights.

In this context, savings and credit is sometimes used as an early intervention to create a sense of identity and shared interest among group members. The analysis of poverty may result in a design for savings and credit provision which concentrates on developing the group's own resources, in terms both of capital, through savings and management, and of group control of the rules and regulations governing the savings and credit systems.

As in the case of SANASA (see 3.4.2), the internal services provided by the group to its members can be quite extensive. This approach promotes internal control over savings and loan funds and is likely to bring about stronger identification with the scheme.

Among the case studies discussed in Chapter 6, URAC in Mexico and ACTIONAID in The Gambia have made institution-building a core component of their approach. URAC is a peasant union whose agenda is economic self-sufficiency in order to reduce the dependency and exploitation which members have experienced in economic relationships. In the course of achieving this the involvement of members in the decision-making structures of the union is vital.

ACTIONAID in the Gambia, on the other hand, sees its credit activities as a means of building up financial resources which village development groups (VDGs) can use to further their own development agenda. Alongside the credit programme there is a programme of training for groups to develop their management and organisation skills.

3.9.2 Social development programmes

Even where the focus is not on enabling groups to manage their own development projects, savings and credit schemes often run alongside programmes of health and literacy. The need for transparency and accountability in financial transactions in such schemes is crucial, but not possible unless members can ensure that records are being properly kept. Sometimes training in literacy and numeracy are a necessary adjunct for a savings and credit programme if there are not enough group members who can fill in their own pass books or keep records. But many literacy programmes in the past have only added numeracy as an afterthought, and failed to provide adequate skills to enable participants to maintain records and ensure accountability. This is part of a wider failure of literacy programmes in general terms. Some new approaches to literacy have succeeded in shifting the balance to more relevant and practical numeracy and literacy skills (Archer and Cottingham, 1996).

3.9.3 Economic development activities

In the past, NGOs have often used savings and credit as part of income-generation programmes. Such interventions have seldom been particularly successful (Mukhopadhyay and March, 1992; Piza Lopez and March, 1990; Riddell and Robinson, 1995). Like savings and credit programmes, this aspect of development work has also been undergoing some re-examination.

Income-generation activities promoted by NGOs have usually concentrated on activities carried out by groups. Problems often resulted from difficulties of organisation and management within the group, as well as from over-optimistic expectations of the income to be generated from the enterprise. This is not to say that there are no successful examples: rather, that these serve to underline the need for internal group cohesion and strong leadership and management, which not all groups possess. People coming together with a common interest of securing a service, such as savings and credit, or working on a common agenda of collective action, can still encounter problems but these are significantly different from the demands of time and energy, often with low returns, arising from a group economic project. The provision of savings and credit to individuals rather than groups has been one of the consequences of this past experience.

The support given to micro-enterprises in terms of business and skills training is often referred to as 'non-financial services'. An argument is now being put forward that such services should be demand-led and self-sustaining (Tanburn, 1996). The rationale behind this contention is that services provided in the past by NGOs (and other providers) have not been particularly useful or appropriate to those trying to set up in business. Therefore if users are not willing to pay for the service, this indicates it is of little real benefit to them.

We argued above that financial management is not necessarily a strong point of NGOs. Likewise, business management is not in general an area in which NGO staff have much direct experience. Therefore it may be more effective for an NGO to encourage entrepreneurs to choose their own training programmes, which the NGO then pays for (with loans if necessary), than to supply a service that is sub-standard.

This strategy would appear to make sense where small businesses are well-developed and have fairly specific needs, and where training opportunities are available, for example, in urban environments. The strategy may encounter greater difficulties where people want to exploit skills or start businesses which do not exist in the area, and they may need additional support to make contacts and visit places where such businesses operate. In such circumstances the role of *promoter* rather than *provider* of support services may be more appropriate for the NGO.

Further considerations for income-generation schemes relate to the economic opportunities already existing in the area. Credit supplied in quantity, where knowledge of what to produce and trading opportunities are limited, can quickly result in market saturation. Supporting moves to experiment and invest in new productive activities may therefore be important.

There may also be good arguments for sharing risks with people as they go about experimenting with new activities. In one of our case studies, CCC in Ecuador, this has been done in the case of a trout-rearing project, an enterprise not known in the area and one which would be far too risky for individuals to take on. However, there is obviously a need to distinguish between supporting experimentation and wasting money, particularly if enterprises are clearly not thriving and individuals have lost interest. Business skills and experience are of great value in making such judgements and NGOs often have a lot to learn from others.

3.10 Summary and conclusions

This chapter has explained and discussed a number of central features in the design of microfinance for poverty reduction. The discussion has sought to illuminate the principles which underlie these features and point out that they need to be combined in different ways in different schemes.

Poverty targeting: many schemes now practise 'self-selection' through keeping loan sizes small, and demanding regular attendance at meetings which better-off people would find time- consuming or socially difficult to attend. However, some schemes still use measures to directly target poor people, such as wealth ranking. 'Self-selection' lowers costs but cannot be assumed to exclude the better-off entirely, especially if loan sizes start to rise as the scheme progresses. Loan size as a feature of targeting can create a dilemma if it prevents poor people ever taking on larger loans.

Women as scheme users: many schemes are designed to provide women with credit. However, it cannot be assumed that disbursing loans to women means either that they use them or that they are empowered. Scheme implementors need to be clear about the gender-related objectives of their intervention and to understand the implications that delivering financial services have for relations between men and women. They should also find ways of supporting women's own strategies for enhancing their position.

Lending through groups: groups have been a common component of methodologies for lending to the poor but repayment does not solely depend on peer pressure; groups take different forms in different contexts and it is important to analyse the mix of circumstances which ensure repayment. This mix goes beyond peer pressure to include supervision, management, transparency, and accountability of the systems.

Savings: voluntary and flexible savings facilities have so far been a largely unmet need of poor people. Interveners should consider developing flexible savings mechanisms. However, to operate a savings facility is to take responsibility for other people's money, and should not be undertaken lightly.

Interest rates: there is now widespread acceptance of the need to charge interest rates which cover inflation and make a contribution to the cost of providing the service. This reassessment has recognised that it is often the availability rather than the cost of credit to poor people which is the constraining factor. Long-term availability requires that the loan fund does not become eroded through inflation, and that a degree of cost-recovery ensures sustainability (see Chapter 4 for further discussion).

- NGOs should understand the design features they incorporate in a scheme in the light of local social and economic circumstances and the objectives of the scheme; there is now a continuously evolving set of design features that can be used in microfinance schemes but no single blueprint for use in all circumstances.

- NGOs should continuously and critically assess design features in the light of the results they produce in practice. This is an important part of impact assessment, as will be discussed in Chapter 5.

4

Financial performance and sustainability

4.1 Introduction

As with any programme intervention, performance monitoring of micro-finance schemes is essential. In the context of managing money the need for timely and accurate information about what is happening cannot be stressed too highly. This chapter does not provide guidelines for financial analysis but emphasises the importance of financial management — an area in which NGOs have tended to be weak. Financial sustainability, which will also be discussed in this chapter, is unlikely to be a feasible objective if financial management is poor.

The ability of some of the best-known institutions which have been operating in this area to gain consistently high repayment rates of 90 per cent and above, and to extend their coverage to relatively large numbers of individuals (see Table 1, Annex 1) has raised expectations that such micro-finance institutions may be able to become sustainable in the long term.

4.2 Managing and assessing financial performance

Managers of a microfinance intervention need to know how well it is performing in financial terms. The first essential is to produce financial statements at the right time. Information that is produced late cannot give an accurate picture of the organisation's financial position. Next, the financial statements must be analysed to produce information about the performance of the scheme which can be used to improve that performance.

The crucial question here is whether the portfolio of loans and savings that the scheme is holding is being effectively managed. We briefly discuss the repayment rate in order to highlight the importance of a proper under-standing and appreciation of the intricacies involved in financial management.

(For more comprehensive guidance on financial management and analysis reference should be made to SEEP, 1995; IADB, 1994; Christen, 1990; and Stearns, 1991.)

4.2.1 The repayment rate

The repayment rate is the indicator most often used as a measure of the performance of a credit scheme (see Annex 2 for an explanation of how it can be calculated). Despite its universality, the way in which the repayment rate is calculated and monitored is not entirely standardised as it must relate to the design of a particular scheme. This means that comparisons across schemes must be undertaken with an awareness of how repayment rates have been calculated.

One of the mistakes that is often made in calculating the repayment rate on loans is that the rate is not clearly defined in relation to a given time period. The figure may therefore include loans which have been made and fully repaid, or it may include repayments which were made after they were due. The amount repaid might include early repayment of their loans made by some borrowers (called 'prepayments'), and these should be excluded from the calculation. Since the repayment rate should precisely measure the ratio of payments made to payments scheduled as due at a particular time, it can also be referred to as the 'on-time' repayment rate.

The different methods used in calculation are well illustrated by the case study schemes set out in Table 6.2, page 88. ACTIONAID in The Gambia calculates its repayment rate as a historical figure reflecting the total amount that has been repaid out of the total ever disbursed. This is a relatively common method but is not standard banking practice and does not indicate the current status of outstanding loans.

4.2.2 Arrears and default

Other indicators, such as default and arrears rates, are also useful financial management information. These indicators monitor the lending portfolio at different points. The arrears rate can capture loans that are past their scheduled time for repayment, i.e. are overdue, and need to be followed up. The default rate includes only those loans which require special action if they are to be recovered. An age analysis of loans outstanding is a standard technique of banking practice. This involves classifying loans in terms of the length of time they are overdue.

Default is a subject that tends to make fieldworkers nervous. They feel that once a borrower knows that a loan is regarded as in default, then he or she will not bother to repay. This reflects the 'soft' approach to repayment in which there are few consequences for non-payment. The classification of a loan as in default should precipitate action on the part of staff of the scheme. At the same time it is vital that the financial health of the scheme is monitored and the intervener knows what proportion of the capital is at risk.

Action to recover loans can also be looked at in the context of other local financial systems. Borrowers who are falling behind with repayments may be indebted to other lenders as well, hence they may set about a rational calculation of which loan it is best for them to default on, based on their own view of the relative merits of different lenders and with which it is most important to retain a good credit record. This is when external schemes, such as those run by NGOs, are likely to encounter problems. The borrower may decide that the NGO is likely to leave the area at some future date, and hence is not likely to be a reliable long-term source of loans. Default on an NGO loan is likely to have less effect on the borrower's local creditworthiness (except in group-based lending systems, where non-payment is public knowledge). The borrower may also think that the NGO has welfare-related objectives and therefore is likely to be more 'understanding'.

It is the syndrome of the 'understanding' NGO, with 'soft' repayment enforcement, which is most likely to lead to the failure of any credit scheme. While the group system of social collateral can provide an added incentive for individual borrowers to repay, there is evidence to suggest that much repayment enforcement is actually carried out by scheme staff. The problem is different if the whole group decides that repayment is not in their interests. This is most likely to occur at the outset of a scheme, when the NGO (if an external one) and the borrowers may not know much about each other. It is because NGOs and other institutions, including governments, have not enforced repayment in the past that the community may collectively decide not to repay. In such cases, if the NGO is serious about the scheme being credit rather than grants, then it must demonstrate this either by taking action to recover loans (for example, asset seizure) or suspending all further loans until existing loans are repaid.

4.3 Financial sustainability

High repayment rates have been reported in schemes where interest rates are high enough to partly cover the costs of providing the services. The circumstances in which long-term financial sustainability might be possible have become a subject for research. A recent study of 11 large established microfinance institutions (Christen, Rhyne and Vogel, 1994) identifies three levels of financial sustainability:

Level 1 *Subsidy dependent:* the costs of the organisation are funded through grants and subsidies from donors.

Level 2 *Operational efficiency:* the non-financial costs of operation (salaries and other administrative costs) are covered out of programme revenues (interest on loans and fees).

Level 3 *Fully self-sufficient* or *profitable:* the institution is generating positive (inflation adjusted) returns on assets. The financial costs of operation are also covered: capital for on-lending is raised through commercial loans and income is enough to cover the costs of these loans.

Ten of the eleven organisations studied had reached level 2, operational efficiency, and five had reached level 3. The study therefore concluded that 'it is consistently possible for competent microfinance programs to achieve *operational* efficiency within a reasonable timeframe' (p.5). However, they are a little more cautious about the potential for full financial self-sustainability, suggesting that 'it remains an open question whether *full* self-sufficiency is consistently possible in a variety of settings' (p.5; authors' emphasis). It is with studies of this type in mind that Otero and Rhyne (1994) propose that 'it is incumbent upon governments and donors that currently support micro-enterprise programmes to demand movement toward viability' (p21).

Discussions of the potential for sustainability sometimes suggest that a microfinance institution can become financially sustainable between seven and ten years after starting operations. Branches of the Grameen Bank can become operationally self-sustaining in the space of five years (Khandker, Khalily and Khan, 1995). Branches of the ASA network in Bangladesh appear to be able to reach this level within eight months of commencing their operations (Rutherford, 1995b). This is achieved by the rapid mobilisation of group ('samity') members and their savings; and the issuing of the first wave of loans within three months of mobilisation. As the ASA branch receives the groups' weekly savings and interest payments it is able to utilise the savings and interest to make more loans, and the interest rates charged allow the salaries of workers to be covered.

4.3.1 The pros and cons of 'scaling up'

Ways of achieving financial sustainability are currently the subject of debate among practitioners. Much emphasis has been put on microfinance operations reaching a sufficiently large number of users so that economies of scale can be made, and the cost of servicing numerous small transactions starts to fall. This emphasis is a cause for concern, as increasing the scale of the operation may become an objective in itself. There are major organisational and management problems to be faced as operations scale up. For many organisations, scaling up may not be appropriate. Two of the schemes described in Chapter 6, URAC in Mexico and Ladywood Credit Union, partly derive their strength from their relatively small scale. For URAC it is the objective of building a peasant union that is important, and the financial services component is one aspect of its work which is contributing to this end; extending its financial services more widely might undermine the core objective. In the case of Ladywood Credit Union, it is the closeness of the service to members, and the time which can be given to helping them address their financial difficulties, which are significant features of the service, and these benefits would be compromised if scaling up was an objective.

A further problem that can arise in the pursuit of financial self-sustainability is that of retaining a focus on the poor. Some organisations find that their users who do well need larger loans over time. This is termed 'graduation', as the users can be seen to be 'graduating' out of the target group which the scheme initially defined. The organisation is then under pressure to increase the size of its loans and continue to work with these people. Although costs per loan fall when loan sizes increase, the disadvantage is that better-off users are likely to be attracted to the services.

The potential for fully self-sufficient microfinance institutions in all settings is questioned in a study of nine interventions in West Africa (Webster and Fidler, 1995). Their findings lead them to believe that while every attempt to move to full cost-recovery should be made, 'the costs of reaching very poor people in remote, rural areas of this region will always exceed possible revenues and [that] subsidies will always be needed to fill the shortfall if the institution is to remain in operation.' A similar conclusion is reached for remote and mountainous areas of Nepal and Pakistan in comparison to more densely populated areas of Bangladesh, Sri Lanka, and India (Bennett, Goldberg and Hunte, 1996). However, Bennett *et al* suggest that it is not only geographical inaccessibility that raises costs but also female seclusion, illiteracy, and poverty.

4.3.2 Issues in sustainability: the experience of 'village banking'

The 'village banking' model illustrates some of the issues in sustainability outlined above. It is a model of financial service delivery set up by the Foundation for International Community Assistance (FINCA), and is employed by a range of NGOs, including Catholic Relief Services, Freedom From Hunger, and Care, in a number of countries.

The original model is one in which a sponsoring agency lends 'seed capital' to a village bank. Village banks ideally consist of between 20 and 50 members. The loan agreement is signed by all members and first loans are for approximately US$50. They are payed back on a weekly basis and the member is also expected to save approximately 20 per cent of the loan during each loan cycle. Loan amounts for clients increase after each one is repaid. Through this process, the village bank is expected to build up its internal capital, pay back the seed capital to the organisation, including interest, and reach internal sustainability within three years.

Experience has been varied but there have been few cases where individual members have been able to 'graduate' to become clients of the formal financial system; nor are there many examples of the village bank itself being able to graduate away from the support of the sponsoring agency to reliance on formal banks alone for loan capital. One of the problems encountered is that members all tend to participate in similar productive activities and hence the demand for loans peaks at a particular time. The need for an external source of capital is therefore crucial and without this the scheme is likely to revert to a rotating savings and credit association. While financial sustainability has been an objective it has not been vigorously pursued. Interest rates have not always been set to cover costs and the detailed accounts which might enable this to happen have not been kept.

The experience suggests there is need for a certain degree of scale and dispersion of loans and savings for financial intermediation to function effectively, and this is unlikely to be found within one village. The theory and the practice have therefore diverged quite significantly, and adjustments and adaptations have been made in implementing the system. While the methodology has demonstrated an ability to reach poor people, and especially women, on whom the programmes have often focused, the vision of financial sustainability is yet to become reality. (Source: Holt, 1994.)

4.3.3 Sustainability through extending coverage

One of the issues raised by this example is the need to operate on a scale larger than village level, since the demand for loans may be simultaneous among a group of people with similar livelihood strategies. Extension of coverage could include wider geographical regions and diverse social groups, which could spread the demand for loans more evenly throughout the year. Ladywood Credit Union is an example of a scheme where better-off members, through taking and repaying loans, support the sustainability of the scheme. The same is true of Casa Campesina Cayambe, where the taking and repaying of loans by relatively wealthier members has enabled the scheme to survive. The difference between LCU and CCC is that the former has made loans only for consumption. Providing bigger loans for productive investment to the relatively wealthier can increase inequality, further skew power relations, and increase relative poverty. Moreover, research for the CCC case-study showed that wealthy households were often the worst repayers. The example of Garu Rural Bank (see 2.8.3) also demonstrates how offering services to local salaried workers such as teachers and civil servants provides the bank with a secure source of income.

It is interesting to consider the sustainability of the informal financial systems described in Chapter 2. Mechanisms such as ROSCAs are financially sustainable since their managerial inputs are voluntary. However, in the course of making procedures more formal, additional costs may arise, such as a salary for a paid manager. Informal schemes also differ in the ways they make use of existing informal structures which may in some cases involve voluntary inputs. A scheme for financial service provision that works with pre-existing ROSCAs may find its costs much lower than one which sets out to establish new groups.

Whether or not financial sustainability is an achievable objective is still the cause of much debate and enquiry, as these experiences illustrate. However, one of the emerging points of consensus is that, even in cases where the scheme is not able to operate in a way that will make it financially sustainable, any subsidy provided by an NGO should be to the operational costs of the scheme rather than in the form of low interest-rates and lax repayment policies. Providing public or donor money to maintain the institution can be viewed as building financial infrastructure. There are some dangers even with this approach, in that access to donor money can lead to a lack of financial discipline on the part of the institution, which may undermine the objective of building up such institutions to survive in the longer term.

4.3.4 Measuring financial sustainability

While the debates described in the previous section continue, NGOs are increasingly being challenged by donors to examine the financial sustainability of their programmes. Exercises of this type can be important in stimulating critical thinking about a programme's direction. Calculating sustainability can be a complex matter but here we will consider two relatively simple measures that can be used to assess where a programme stands financially: the sustainability index and the break-even interest rate.

Sustainability index

A straightforward way to look at the financial sustainability of the savings and credit operation is to look at its income compared to its costs (Havers, 1996).

Sustainability Index (SI) = Percentage of total costs covered by income

$$= \frac{\text{total income earned from credit programme during the period}}{\text{total credit programme costs during period}} \times 100$$

The income received includes interest and fees on loans. Programme costs include all staff, office, and other costs necessary to run the programme. It is suggested that even costs which are not directly incurred should be included for the purposes of this calculation. For example, if office space is free because of a special arrangement, a figure for notional rent should be included, so that the programme can be evaluated as if it had to cover all its costs out of income.

However, in schemes where inputs are voluntary and likely to continue into the future, there is a case to be made for not including these costs in the calculation of financial sustainability. In Chapter 6 we discuss the example of the Ladywood Credit Union in the UK in which volunteers provide much of the labour. This is a characteristic of the project and it would therefore be inappropriate to suggest that the project was not financially sustainable as a credit union because of this free labour.

It must be stressed that the loan fund and savings deposits are not part of this calculation. However, if the loan fund has been received from donors as a grant, the calculation should include an imputed cost for this (i.e. the interest that it would be necessary to pay if the funds were to be raised from another source). The interest rate charged by banks in the formal sector is often used to calculate this cost. The purpose of including such a cost is to make clear the dependence of the scheme on donors or other sources of subsidised capital.

Attempting such a calculation demonstrates the benefits of keeping savings and credit scheme accounts separate from those of other activities. In cases where staff are shared between programme activities it is necessary to make an estimate of staff time and resources spent on the savings and credit component. Overleaf is an example of the calculation for one of the case-study schemes, URAC in Mexico.

The calculation is presented for URAC on the basis of 1995 figures. It is an illustration only and is not intended actually to portray the sustainability of URAC.

Costs		N$
75% of salary costs of 4 development workers [1]		248,850
Operational costs [2]		96,060
Computers — estimated depreciation		6,500
Main office utilities		1,756
Main office maintenance		4,000
Vehicle — petrol		18,000
Vehicle — maintenance		14,000
Vehicle — depreciation		15,400
Interest paid on savings		163,996
	Total costs	568,562

Income		
Interest received on loans and bank interest on deposits		268,395
	Total income	268,395

Calculation of SI:

$$\frac{\text{Income}}{\text{Costs}} \times 100 = 47\%$$

Notes:

1 These figures are based on estimates of the proportion of vehicle use and development workers' time devoted to the savings and credit part of URAC's work. It is estimated that the development workers spend 75 per cent of their time on the savings and credit programme and the remainder on their other activities.

2 Operational costs include: clerical salaries, stationery and other consumables, bank commission, free gifts, transport to committee meetings (for cashiers) and the costs of the mobile office.

In the case of URAC it has not been necessary to estimate a cost for the loan fund because it is generated from savings and hence is being paid for by paying interest on savings. This calculation of the sustainability index demonstrates that URAC is covering 47 per cent of the costs incurred in running the scheme out of income generated through its own operations. This means that in order to continue its operations if donor funds were withdrawn it would have to either double its income or halve its costs or both. The strategies for raising income would include raising the interest rate on loans and charging fees for certain services or transactions. The major element of cost is clearly salaries of the development workers and currently these staff are essential to the integrity of the programme.

The break-even interest rate
An alternative approach to looking at financial sustainability is to calculate the interest rate that the scheme would have to charge its borrowers if it had no source of income other than interest income and fees. This is referred to as the break-even interest rate. If the rate turns out to be extremely high compared to the formal sector and local informal rates, it is likely that the demand for the scheme's loans would collapse and it would have to adjust its operations to survive. Below is an example of the calculation for URAC.

Total costs incurred in 1995 were N$568,562. The loan volume in 1995 was N$749,000. For the purposes of this calculation we will assume that this figure represents an average volume of loans outstanding at any point during the year. The interest paid by URAC on savings is included in the costs (see previous calculation).

On the basis of these figures, URAC would have to charge an interest rate of 76 per cent on the N$749,000 of loans it has outstanding in order to bring in income of N$568,562; 76 per cent is therefore the break-even interest rate. This compares with the current interest rate charged of 30 per cent. In the economic situation in Mexico in 1995 formal bank interest rates ranged from 50 to 70 per cent. The break-even rate for URAC would appear to compare quite well with such rates. However, those rates in the commercial sector caused massive rates of default on the part of middle-class households; and whether URAC's clients could cope with such levels is open to question.

However, separating the costs of fieldworkers and management time between savings and credit activities and other programmes as in this calculation does not necessarily mean that the organisational form which this implies would be viable. Since at present programme activities are integrated and costs shared, the removal of funded components might mean that the way in which groups and service delivery are organised would not be sustainable.

4.4 Managerial and organisational sustainability

Even if it was clear that the organisation was able to cover its operating costs, this would be only one factor in moving a savings and credit scheme towards an independent future. The structure and management of the organisation are equally important considerations.

NGOs do not necessarily possess the most appropriate skills for managing financial services. As well as carrying out regular and efficient financial monitoring, the management of the scheme must demonstrate integrity and accountability in dealing with other people's money. (It is only necessary to consider what type of organisation you, the reader, would trust with your own money to understand some of the qualities needed.)

4.4.1 The role of staff in microfinance interventions

One of the critical issues is staffing. Not only is it important that staff feel motivated to undertake the intensive supervision that most financial services programmes entail, but the honesty and integrity of the institution and its staff in dealing with the funds must be apparent. Without this, the credibility of the organisation in the eyes of its users will soon suffer and demand for services will decline.

Jain (1996) describes how, in the case of Grameen, group meetings promote the transparency and accountability of staff as well as members. Members can see that funds are not being mishandled and claims from individuals to their entitlements under the scheme are not being denied. Experience in Casa Campesina Cayambe revealed that when procedures for loan application only required the approval of the Credit Delegate, a very small number of cases occurred in which he would require 'fees' for non-existent administration or a percentage of the loan. As a result the policy was changed to involve three members of the community in supporting loan applications. The transparency which village meetings can promote benefits the users by helping to control the behaviour of scheme staff or volunteers. It is also necessary to prevent staff colluding with scheme users to abuse the scheme. In the case of Ladywood Credit Union, interlocking committees made up of staff and members check on each other.

One of the most important debates in this context is how to structure staff remuneration and incentives. Some schemes offer incentives for loan collection related to the performance of the groups with which a staff member works. There is a danger that quantitative performance targets of this kind may lead to a neglect of institution-building among members (Montgomery, 1995), which is fundamental to sustainability. In the case of URAC, group cashiers at first worked on an entirely voluntary basis. They were offered an incentive in the form of a points system related to the supply of basic goods, which was another element of the programme. This has resulted in co-operation among them to improve the quality of the record-keeping on behalf of the group. As such it is an example of an incentive that has been structured in a way which improves the capacity of the cashiers and hence the institution-building objectives of the project as a whole, as well as contributing to the efficient running of the scheme.

For NGO workers who interact daily with users, often on a wide range of issues, becoming debt-collectors on behalf of a savings and credit scheme can put them in a difficult position, and it is this tension that has so often in the past led to a 'soft' approach by NGOs interested in poverty alleviation. Staff may find themselves in an ambiguous relationship with users which impairs performance.

4.4.2 Organisational sustainability and change

Effective management also requires continuous adaptation and change on the part of those in control. Circumstances are continually changing: macroeconomic conditions, legal requirements, the needs of users, and the availability of other financial services in the area. All of these changes mean that the scheme must continually adapt its operations as new information comes to light and experience is built up. Flexibility is essential. (See Chapter 5 for a discussion of adaptability as an indicator of impact.)

In Chapter 2 we argued that financial services are not something which should be here today and gone tomorrow. If providing them is to make a significant contribution to the alleviation of poverty, a long-term approach is needed. The organisational framework which will enable this future sustainability must be considered.

Throughout this book we have discussed a range of different organisational forms: ROSCAs, village banks, credit unions (SANASA and Ladywood), schemes run and managed by NGOs itself (AATG, URAC, SUNGI and CCC), and organisations which have the status of banks (BRI and Grameen Bank). These projects offer a rich and diverse range of experience from which to draw in considering what forms of organisation might be most appropriate and enduring.

The most obvious organisational form for sustained financial service provision is a bank, and we have given two examples of organisations that started out as banks: BRI (a state-owned bank) on a very large scale in Indonesia and Garu Rural Bank on a much smaller scale in Northern Ghana. Two organisations, BancoSol in Bolivia and Grameen in Bangladesh, started out as NGOs and have been able to convert themselves into banks, which might suggest that this is a course of action many more schemes should follow. However, the feasibility of this approach for other organisations in other circumstances is in question. Grameen had to gain unique governmental dispensation to convert itself into a bank, whereas BRAC has so far been unsuccessful in obtaining a similar concession.

Apart from legal difficulties of this type, some commentators do not agree that such a process should be an objective of NGOs, believing 'that the competitive advantage of NGOs is in their capacity to reach the poorest and engage in activities which help people change, but which cannot necessarily be financially supported by the recipient of the assistance' (Dichter, 1996). Dichter concluded that NGOs should concentrate on what they do best rather than trying to become banks. Such debates are unlikely to be easily resolved. Meanwhile, NGOs with microfinance interventions are considering how they might establish organisations that are able to survive. Legal status is clearly one of the main concerns, and we have argued above the need for government regulation of organisations taking deposits (see Chapter 3). The major legally-recognised alternative to banks is the credit union.

Credit unions, in being owned by their members and savings-based, present two characteristics for survival that the above discussions have shown to be particularly important, and which NGOs may feel to be strongly convergent with their own values. However, there is still much to be learned in this area, and many countries have no legislation or regulations to deal with credit unions.

An alternative strategy for NGOs is to persuade national banks and private financial institutions to extend their services to poor people. Groups with whom the NGO has developed a relationship can then be encouraged to transfer their custom to a sympathetic bank, so removing the need for the NGO to provide long-term support. Another role for NGOs is to engage with governments in discussing how the financial needs of the poor can best be addressed. Organisations such as Women's World Banking, for example, have worked to raise the issue with governments and policy makers (WWB, 1994).

4.5 Summary and conclusions

This chapter has emphasised the critical importance of continuous monitoring of financial performance. Financial sustainability should be explored, using some relatively simple calculations which, even if not entirely accurate, can give an impetus to debate about the future of the programme. However, financial sustainability should not be seen solely within the context of this narrow financial calculation, in which, for example, voluntary inputs such as labour are costed. Some organisations are fully capable of sustaining the flow of such voluntary inputs, which can be integral to the achievement of their objectives.

Even within the context of debates about financial self-sustainability there are questions about whether it is achievable, especially where there is low population density, or where physical constraints, such as poor infrastructure and communication, and social constraints, such as illiteracy and female seclusion, increase the costs of delivering services. These factors reduce the likelihood of being able to recover costs through charging appropriate interest rates.

Financial sustainability is only one component of ensuring that schemes are able to provide services in the long term; aspects of management and organisational structure are equally critical. The organisational form may be the most significant design element in relation to long-term sustainability. Some NGOs have turned themselves into banks, but this is not likely to be an option for most NGOs.

Pressures for financial self-sustainability are likely to produce dilemmas for the organisation. An institution which increases loan size may lose its focus on poor people; the strategy of deliberately including better-off people in order to subsidise lending to the very poor requires a clear organisational vision if it is to succeed.

- The monitoring and management of financial information is a specialist area and should be recognised as such by building the necessary skills among NGO staff or using outside specialists.

- Considerations of sustainability in both organisational and financial terms need to be made from the outset; but even when a project is already underway prospects for financial and organisational sustainability should be addressed.

- In order to develop a sustainable organisation within the national regulatory framework it may be necessary to undertake advocacy work to change existing government policies.

- The progress of the institution towards financial and organisational sustainability is not the sole indicator of achievement. For organisations with an agenda for poverty reduction, assessing the impact of the services on users is crucial. This is the subject of the next chapter.

5

Assessing impact

5.1 Introduction

As we have seen in the last two chapters, microfinance technology can take many forms, and interventions with microfinance components have been designed in varied ways. This chapter is concerned with understanding how the consequences of microfinance interventions can be measured and attributed. If financial service provision has had poverty reduction as a goal, it is particularly important to know whether, by how much, and for whom poverty has reduced (or increased) and the extent to which these changes have occurred as a result of the intervention.

The chapter begins by discussing conventional approaches to measuring impact and explores some of their methodological and practical problems. NGOs have made substantial progress in promoting alternative methods of collecting information. The third section draws on this new body of work in examining ways of overcoming some of the problems associated with conventional impact assessment. A crucial source of information is users' own accounts of the usefulness and relevance of the services in supporting their livelihoods. In the fourth section, it is suggested that rather than addressing impact as a question to be answered only once, usually after an intervention has been made, the relevance and usefulness of services should be continually assessed. Through this learning process, the organisation can adapt its services to better meet the needs of users.

5.2 The difficulties of assessing impact

Development project managers and their funders have long engaged in linear thinking about the consequences of their actions. *Inputs*, in terms of people, resources and activities, lead to *outputs* which themselves have *outcomes*. These outcomes have an *impact* on people, often a targeted group. In order to demonstrate to themselves, their donors, and supporters that their work is proceeding as planned, organisations endeavour to assess the impact of their activities.

It is particularly important for organisations like Oxfam and ACTIONAID to understand the impact of their work. They each rely on support from large numbers of voluntary donors, who give money on the basis that it will be used to further the organisation's mission. Oxfam's Mission Statement refers to 'working with poor people....in their struggle against hunger, disease, exploitation and poverty'. Such a commitment to poor people implies that Oxfam should also be accountable to *them* for its actions. Indeed, for NGOs in general, it has been argued that impact assessment is important in enabling them to remain true to their mission; and that poor quality impact assessment is likely to leave them more vulnerable to co-option by others (Edwards and Hulme, 1995).

Yet poor people 'are not static "targets" waiting to be "impacted" upon by credit programs' (Abdullah, Rutherford and Hossain, 1995). People's actions, ducking and weaving through structural constraints and opportunities, have their own consequences. These actions, whether freely chosen or not, can combine with the processes and outcomes of planned intervention to enhance or diminish well-being. Interventions, generally less nimble, continue, and outcomes and impact over time are very difficult to predict. How, then, should NGOs measure the impact of their work?

In Chapter 1 we outlined three ways of defining poverty: lack of income, vulnerability to income fluctuations, and powerlessness. Interventions could attempt to reduce poverty by raising incomes (income promotion); increasing income and livelihood security (protection); or empowering people who lack control and choice in their lives. Impact assessment of NGO-funded financial services has usually focused on the first of these: income promotion. Emphasis has been placed on measuring changes in income levels following credit programmes, especially those where loans have been directed to specific uses. This approach raises a number of methodological problems especially where the impact of *directed* credit is being assessed:

- respondents may give false information if loans have been used for a purpose other than the stipulated one;

- establishing a causal relationship to the actual loan in question involves knowledge of all the beneficiary's sources and uses of funds;

- it is difficult to establish what would have happened if the loan had not been made (Mansell-Carstens, 1995).

5.2.1 Establishing loan use

The first of these dilemmas has at its heart the 'fungibility' of cash, that is, the potential for funds to be used for purposes other than those stated. Micro-finance interveners may or may not insist that loans be used in certain ways. If they do impose conditions for loan use, they may find themselves wasting resources trying to discover if these have been fulfilled. As ACTIONAID Vietnam (AAV) lament in the proposal for an impact evaluation methodology for their Son La Programme, 'in practice it is very difficult to determine the use to which fungible loans are put. It would be interesting to know whether the microfinance activities have enabled households to improve food security or to invest in a profitable activity, but AAV does not consider that a loan use survey is likely to generate conclusive information on this' (1996). For these reasons, the village-level research for the case study of SUNGI in Pakistan (see Chapter 6), focused much more on asking respondents to compare streams of income with the size of repayment instalments than on attempting to determine whether loan use was as stated on the application form.

However, similar problems arise when poverty is defined in broader terms, and when credit is not directed to specific uses. Investigators carrying out one-off impact assessments rarely have the time to talk to people for long enough to find out the complexity of their livelihood strategies and the details of how they manage their finances. (This was also true of the assessments attempted for this book which could not by their very nature involve long-term engagement.) In addition, respondents themselves have little incentive to discuss their personal finances openly. People may disguise the real purpose to which loans were put for fear of offending project staff; or because they believe that action may be taken against them; or because they calculate a possible advantage in doing so; or simply because to do so can be quite amusing in the course of a boring interview.

5.2.2 Measuring change: controls and baselines

A related and more general difficulty is that of establishing from respondent recall the changes that have occurred over time as the result of an intervention. One of the major problems here is the relationship of both researcher and respondent to the microfinance institution itself. Both have interests in the outcome of the impact assessment. For example, a respondent might want a further loan and think that a positive story about the way a previous loan had improved her or his life might help to get that loan. Similarly, an investigator hoping for re-employment might not wish to offend the agency hiring her. It is very difficult to establish what would have happened in the absence of a loan. For quantitative analysis a control is required: a sample of people, similar in every other way, who have not received a loan, compared with a sample who have. As well as being costly and time-consuming, to establish a perfect control is virtually impossible (Copestake, 1996b).

An alternative to using a control group is to use a baseline against which to assess change. Unfortunately, good baseline data rarely exist. Experience with quantitative baseline surveys of household income and assets has shown that it is costly and difficult to collect adequate data. Such surveys often raise as many questions as they answer, and staff who originally collected the data may no longer be available to explain the intricacies of the data when it comes to using them to answer questions about impact. Moreover, if project objectives have changed in the course of time, the original baseline data will give an inappropriate or irrelevant picture of the pre-project situation; for this reason, some information can only be collected at the end of a project (Newens and Roche, 1996).

Capturing the unintended impacts of interventions is also problematic. We have argued in Chapter 2 for the importance of looking at an intervention in the context of other locally available services. If 'enabling' aspects of these existing services have actually been undermined by an intervention, then this information also needs to be part of the assessment of impact. A further unplanned impact may occur if the provision of credit to one group allows them to invest in a particular market opportunity, with the result that established producers or traders are displaced.

The concepts of 'controls' and 'baselines' also raise moral questions for interveners. What do people gain from spending time monitoring or being monitored for the impact on them of *not* being beneficiaries of a project? One possible solution to this problem is to include new users as the 'control' group, and to use recall to make comparisons with how things were before the intervention.

5.2.3 Proving causality

A final and major obstacle is the difficulty in being able to attribute any change that is found to the intervention. Other events and changes occur while the intervention is taking place, and this may make it virtually impossible to separate out the impact of a savings and credit programme. Further, even if apparently successful in terms of raising incomes, reducing vulnerability or challenging unequal power relations, an intervention may make very little difference to people's overall well-being. The positive changes may be dwarfed or negated by other factors in the local context or by macro-economic or political changes, and therefore be marginal. This points to the need to frame objectives of what can be achieved by providing financial services, in more modest terms.

5.3 Innovations in impact assessment

The response of many microfinance specialists to the methodological and practical difficulties of impact assessment has been to argue that it should not be attempted at all. Rather, the financial health of the microfinance institution should be taken as a proxy indicator of positive change. They argue that the very popularity of the services among poor people is enough to demonstrate that they find the services of benefit.

It has been suggested, therefore, that impact studies should be replaced by indicators of scale and institutional sustainability (Rhyne, 1994). If the institution is increasing the outreach of its services to a growing number of people, and indicators of financial sustainability are improving, the impact of the institution is viewed as positive. However, while the fact that increasing numbers of people are using the services is in itself a positive indication, it does not tell enough of the story. Aside from the fact that increasing scale brings its own problems, and can even undermine the sustainability of the institution itself, as discussed earlier in this book, it is necessary to investigate further to find out *who* is using the services. Users should be differentiated by wealth, gender, and location; and information should be gathered on *how* various groups are using the services to support their livelihood activities. Understanding how people use the services in practice makes it possible to analyse what makes them *relevant and useful* to poor people.

Answers to the question of whether relatively better-off or poorer people are using the services can be found by undertaking wealth-ranking exercises with members and non-members (Pretty *et al*, 1996). Discussions with them in 'focus groups' can reveal their views on why others do not join the scheme or why they may have dropped out. Following up users who may have dropped out or become inactive is particularly helpful in understanding why the scheme may not be able to meet these users' needs, as are interviews with non-members. It may be that a member has dropped out because her income-earning husband has died, or her son has stopped sending back remittances from outside the area. This would raise the question of how financial services can support her in dealing with this situation. Or perhaps discussions with non-users might uncover difficulties for in-migrants to an area in being accepted in groups which rely on social collateral.

We have earlier emphasised the distinction between *access* to and *use* of scheme services. When considering who is using services, it again becomes important to understand women's roles, particularly in relation to loans.

Female members may be able to describe the process of decision making before and after taking the loan, their role in it, and how they felt about it. How repayments are made, and how women who may not have direct access to income develop strategies for ensuring repayment, are essential aspects of appreciating the relevance of the services to them. For example, women in Bangladesh often find the money to make weekly compulsory savings deposits required for group membership by taking a handful of rice from the daily household allocation and saving this up to sell (White, 1991).

To assess how services are relevant and useful to users and to what extent requires answers to a range of questions: how users see them in the context of other locally available services; how the amounts and timing of loans and ease of withdrawals from savings accounts relate to their priorities in meeting consumption needs and production opportunities (across seasons); how repayment schedules and any compulsory savings deposits relate to flows of income available to individuals and the household as a whole.

The views of a range of users can be elicited via semi-structured interviews (Pretty *et al*, 1995). However, questions need to be carefully framed, so that respondents are encouraged to share their experience of using the services, and how the services relate to their circumstances. For example, asking 'Why did you withdraw savings at this time?' or 'Why did you take a loan at this time?' might result in more useful responses than questions such as 'What did you use your savings for?' or 'How did you use this loan?' (ACTIONAID Vietnam, 1996).

5.3.1 Researching usefulness: a case study

The following account of research into the usefulness of locally available financial services in The Gambia can illustrate many of the points raised:

> *During case study field work in The Gambia, preference ranking was used to understand better how AATG's credit programme related to other sources of credit available to the villagers. As AATG knew little about how villagers saved, a discussion of the advantages and disadvantages of various types of savings proved illuminating.*
>
> *Research was carried out sometimes with women only, but usually with both women and men. As the researchers moved from village to village, they became more adept at ensuring the women's participation in a mixed group discussion. The discussions took about two hours and were facilitated by two field workers, who began by asking about the different sources of credit available to people. Since villagers often emphasised formal sources and failed to mention their own group systems it was usually necessary to ask probing*

*questions to find out about the latter. Then advantages and
disadvantages of these sources were discussed.*

*For example, in the village of Jiffarong, sources of credit included
The Gambia Co-operative Union Ltd, Village Savings and Credit
Association (VISACA), Freedom From Hunger Campaign (FFHC),
Co-operative consumer shop, and the Department of Community
Development (DCD), as well as the AATG Group Revolving Fund.
The Co-operative had provided three carts to its members to carry
farm produce, people, and goods to and from the village. The Co-
operative Society used to provide cash credit for subsistence purposes
but no longer did so. Only registered members who sell their produce
(usually groundnuts) to the Society could obtain credit and the
majority of members are men. The Co-op applied strict measures
in their credit-recovery programmes, and this discouraged farmers
from applying for credit.*

*Some time ago FFHC also supplied three carts on credit to some
community members and provided some production inputs on a
small scale. The VISACA has been newly introduced and provides
cash credit, but also with stringent loan-recovery measures. A village
bank has been built through VISACA where registered members and
the VDG are able to deposit savings and gain interest. The DCD also
provided one cart to the village some years ago but no longer provides credit in kind.*

*Funds from the Group Revolving Fund had been used for the
purchase of basic commodities such as rice, sugar, and oil which
were supplied to members during the time of food shortage. The
group members also borrowed cash from the GRF to buy seeds for
planting, to be repaid during the course of the trading season.
Part of the GRF was also used to set up a village bakery to generate
income. The consumer shop set up by the group also provides some
savings and credit facilities to its members. The group has saved the
sum of D2300 ($230)which yielded an interest of D232 ($23) over
a one-year period.*

5.3.2 Assessing impact on social relationships

There are other questions which might be asked about the dynamics that the
intervention itself can catalyse:

- Is social differentiation (inequality) and thus *relative* poverty increasing as
  a direct or indirect result of the intervention?

- Do gains in financial security and material well-being by relatively better-off people among the poor increase practices of exploitation and exclusion of even poorer people?

- Can the impact of an intervention *inside* poor households be identified?

- If services are not used by the poorest people are there other resources and services which should be made available for them?

Who is using the service and what happens as a result is a function of social relations which can themselves change *as a result* of financial services interventions. Yaqub (1995) has shown convincingly how attempting to use peer-group pressure to screen borrowers and enforce repayment can have unintended consequences if the lending organisation is unaware of changes within social institutions. Referring to the experience of BRAC in Bangladesh, Yaqub argues that the very empowerment which repeated borrowing can bring to an individual may turn a good repayer into a defaulter. Over time, wealth differences emerge *within the group* and the social sanctions imposed on a defaulting group member may become less threatening: the member has less to lose by letting down the group if she has built up her own resource base. Yaqub uses this to support the case for a permanent subsidy for institution-building at the group level. If the intervention is enabling empowerment of its members, it will become more difficult for the groups on which its success is based to function, and work will be needed to maintain group solidarity.

5.3.3 Impact assessment as a dynamic process

It is clear that the usefulness of financial services varies over time, as well as between different groups of people, as can be seen in the varying use made of those services. The example given in Chapter 2 of a study of low-income people from diverse ethnic backgrounds in the UK illustrates this point. Each group mixed formal and informal financial services in different ways. The financial institutions to which people already had access seemed to affect the demand for new financial services.

The implications of this are that it is necessary to engage in continuing dialogue with a representative cross-section of scheme members, who are likely to have different needs and uses for the services (women and men, landed and landless, different ethnic groups, and so on). Such a process should be designed to ensure that all relevant views are gathered. It should allow the 'facts' to be cross-checked and thus overcome the problem of respondents giving false information. Also, by collecting multiple views of performance the chances of establishing *causality* are increased. The way in which this monitoring process is designed should enable conflicts of interest between different users to emerge and less powerful as well as more powerful people to speak freely. Then rather than looking in a linear way at intentions versus outcomes, performance standards can be set according to 'the criteria or factors which relevant people are likely to use when making a judgement' (Fowler, 1995).

5.3.4 Validating qualitative data

A process approach such as this, which relies heavily on qualitative information collected through methods such as semi-structured interviews and focus group discussions with users, can appear arbitrary and is often criticised for this reason. However, it can be made more rigorous by paying attention to the process involved and being able to evaluate the validity of the information. Pretty (1994) has suggested criteria and characteristics for judging the trustworthiness of data generated through qualitative enquiry, which include:

- **prolonged engagement:** with users so that trust can build up over time;

- **observation:** both of users' behaviour in relation to the services and of the context in which this happens;

- **cross-checking:** (triangulation) of information by using multiple sources of information, multiple ways of finding out that information, and a number of investigators;

- **analysis of difference:** allowing a wide range of perspectives to be brought into the analysis and not necessarily seeking consensus;

- **making use of negative findings:** allowing findings which do not meet with expectations to revise the results and reformulate the expectations, rather than dismissing such findings as exceptions;

- **peer checking:** exposing analysis to colleagues not involved in the enquiry at an early stage and continuing to do so in order to expose biases or assumptions which might remain implicit;

- **checking the data with users:** after collecting information using participatory approaches, checking the interpretation with those from whom the information was collected and so establishing its credibility as representing users' actual views;

- **giving reports:** explaining hypotheses about impact and the context in which they have been developed, and using direct quotations of people's personal experiences and detailed descriptions of context to substantiate these reports;

- **keeping reflexive journals:** recognising the central role played by investigators themselves, they use these journals to record information about themselves, their feelings, and decisions; journals need not be shared with others but can be used at a later stage to remember the immediate reasons for methodological decisions and interpretation of data;

- **conducting an inquiry audit:** this should be carried out by someone unconnected to the inquiry who looks at the process followed and the results to confirm that the findings are supported by the data and are internally coherent.

Our suggested approach to impact assessment focuses on understanding who uses the services on offer, and in what ways those services are relevant and useful to poor people in supporting their livelihoods. 'Relevance' and 'usefulness' are highly subjective, so criteria such as those proposed by Pretty can be important in adding credibility and legitimacy to findings.

Nevertheless, as White has argued 'sharing through participation does not necessarily mean sharing in power' (1996, p6). The relationship between the interests of the donor agency or implementing organisation in establishing whether it is reaching its overall goals, and the interests of its users in addressing the same question, is an unequal one. Information from impact assessment exercises can be ignored if inconvenient, or can be used for political purposes inside an organisation. On the other hand, for an organisation which is based on attracting savings, users have ownership rights in a very real sense, and the organisation should pay great attention to users' assessments.

5.3.5 Using quantitative data in impact assessment

The ways in which members use services can be explored and cross-checked using quantitative as well as qualitative data. Computerised management-information systems are important for the efficient and timely generation of quantitative data. It should be possible to analyse the following information:

- **savings behaviour:** size, frequency and timing of deposits and withdrawals;

- **savings balances:** size of balance held by different categories of people: women, men, better-off, poorer, etc;

- **loan sizes and types** taken, when and by whom;

- **repayment performance** of different categories of people.

This information can be analysed in relation to aspects of the local economy and livelihood systems to further establish how useful and relevant the services are to particular groups of people. For example, the timing of savings and loan activities could be analysed in relation to local events such as agricultural seasonality, festivals, and so on. A good database should enable creative use of the data to be made in answering a range of questions. If records are kept at the level of the individual borrower then it is possible to examine the number of loans that have been taken by each borrower. This allows the extent to which people are making repeated use of the service to be analysed. For example, finding out whether loan sizes are rising or falling with second or third loans can provide insight into borrowers' confidence, or lack of it, in taking larger or smaller loans. Analysing the timing of savings withdrawals in relation to loan disbursement may indicate whether savings are only being made in order to obtain loans.

5.4 Learning and adaptability

To develop a package of services which responds to a specific context requires a willingness to learn and to change. It requires a good information flow between all those 'stakeholders' involved: users, staff, management, and funders. Assessment must be continuous because people, their circumstances, and their aspirations change. The extent to which an organisation learns from experience and adapts accordingly can itself be used as a measure of success. Indicators could be, for example, how well an organisation listens both to users and funders; how efficiently it learns and adapts as a result; and the degree to which it rewards learning and innovation (Roche, 1995).

Changing organisational practice to encourage learning and adaptation has obvious advantages in that it increases the likelihood that mistakes will be admitted and corrective action taken. However, any process approach of this nature can be used to support changes which are more to do with satisfying the interests of particular, already powerful, people — whether management, staff or particular groups of users — than with a focus on successful poverty reduction.

Moreover, learning, adaptability, and understanding must take into account the wider environment in which the institution operates and not be confined to the organisation's own services. Microfinance institutions, user-owned or otherwise, need good sources of information on the nature of and changes in other financial services institutions locally. As Howes has concluded for membership organisations in general;

> ... *successful outcomes nearly always seem to rest, in the first instance, on a sound understanding of existing institutions.*

A capacity to identify and utilise present sources of social capital[1]
*can often give new initiatives a head start. Conversely, where the
institutions which are in place constitute part of the problem to be
addressed, a thorough knowledge of how they operate is indispens-
able as a means of anticipating and managing the conflicts which
will inevitably arise* (Howes, 1996).

Perhaps because of the inherent difficulties of gathering so much information and keeping in touch with changes;

*... NGOs should start slowly, pilot-testing new ideas carefully with
small groups of people ... Institutional development is a long-term
undertaking, and strategy must be harnessed to a process approach
to ensure flexibility in the light of evolving external circumstances*
(Howes, op. cit.).

1 'Social capital' refers to the networks, relationships and mutual obligations which
lie behind collective action and exchange.

5.5 Summary and conclusions

We have discussed the failings of conventional approaches to impact assessment which have taken a linear view of the relationship between an intervention and its consequences. These approaches encounter methodological and practical problems when put into practice. Problems include the difficulties of getting accurate data, and whether the consequences observed can in fact be attributed to the intervention in question.

In recent years substantial progress has been made in developing methodologies which involve users more deeply, in order to capture the diversity of experience which exists among them. Such approaches to impact assessment do not necessarily assume that services will have a measurable impact, but instead seek to increase understanding of the ways in which the services are relevant and useful in supporting users' livelihood strategies.

Approaches which involve continuing engagement with users in a more dynamic dialogue make it possible to meet their needs more effectively. At the same time, if done well, they have the potential to enhance users' identification with the institution, and are therefore in the interests of that institution and its funders. Impact assessment becomes a process of continuous feedback rather than a one-off exercise.

- NGOs interested in poverty reduction should be concerned with the impact of financial services, and especially loans, on poor people's livelihoods.

- In addressing the question of impact, NGOs need to go beyond quantitative information detailing the numbers of users, and volumes and sizes of loans disbursed, to an understanding of how and for whom these services support livelihoods.

- In using qualitative methods to understand the usefulness and relevance of services to poor people, NGOs should develop ways of increasing the trustworthiness of data, by involving a wide range of both users and staff in the process.

- An NGO which is modest and honest in setting its initial objectives, and which is prepared to admit its mistakes and learn from them, is more likely to provide services which are useful and relevant to a wide range of users and so have a more significant impact in supporting their livelihoods.

6

Case studies

6.1 Introducing the case studies

The purpose of this chapter is to explore further the concepts and approaches already laid out in earlier chapters through discussion of five case studies of microfinance interventions. Each case study is presented thematically in terms of its background, design, performance and sustainability, and impact assessment to correspond to the four preceding chapters. Tables 6.1 and 6.2 present information in summary form on the background, design and performance of all five microfinance interventions. Each case study is then discussed in detail. Information on impact was gathered using brief one-off studies. While an attempt was made in each case to assess the usefulness and relevance of the financial services, it was not possible to use all the methodologies for impact assessment advocated in Chapter 5. This was because the approach to learning and adaptation set out in that chapter requires long-term processes involving users, staff, and volunteers.

The five examples discussed are connected with ACTIONAID and Oxfam (UK and Ireland). The Union Regional de Apoyo Campesino in Mexico has received modest financial support from the Mexico programme of Oxfam (UK and Ireland) for a number of years. SUNGI in Pakistan has worked with Oxfam Pakistan, although not in microfinance activities. The study of Ladywood Credit Union in Birmingham UK has been done jointly for the purposes of this book and as a preliminary study for Oxfam's recently established UK programme. ACTIONAID has been working in The Gambia since 1979, and this provides an example of a long-term project where an international NGO has been directly operational. Casa Campesina Cayambe in Ecuador has been a partner project of ACTIONAID and Ayuda en Accion since 1988.

Table 6.1 Summary of Information about Case Study Schemes

	Mexico Union Regional de Apoyo Campesino (URAC)	**Pakistan** SUNGI Development (SUNGI)
National GDP per capita (US$ 1993)	3,610	430
Location	Rural	Rural
Definition of intended users/size	Rural households in 26 communities	47 villages
Scheme membership	4591 active members (1995)	1260 saving; 137 borrowing
Savings facilities	Voluntary savings: savings balance must be 20% of loan size	Compulsory: Rs30 per month minimum
Loan facilities	General purpose 'normal' loan max N$700 (US$100) over 7 months; also loans for housing, family purposes and small-scale agricultural production	Max Rs 5000 (US$150) for productive purposes for 6–24 months
Interest rates (%): Savings: nominal real	18 (note 1)	profit-loss share
Loans: nominal real	30 (note 1)	18 (service charge) 8
Way of working (through individuals or groups)	20–70 members organised for savings purposes with one cashier; loans signed by 5–10 other members	Village Organisations, men and women separately, size variable. Has credit management committee

1   Inflation rates in Mexico have fluctuated significantly in the last two years resulting in both positive and negative rates in real terms, currently rates have become significantly positive again but were not at the time which the study was undertaken

UK Ladywood Credit Union (LCU)	Gambia ACTIONAID The Gambia (AATG)	Ecuador Casa Campesina Cayambe (CCC)
18,060	350	1,200
Urban	Rural	Rural
Unemployed / low-income and other families on inner-city housing estates	Small farmers / rural households in 523 villages	Small farmers / rural households of 2 cantons with a population of 3,150 families
270 adults 400 junior savers	Approx. 11,000 households have received credit to date	Individual coverage figures not available
Voluntary: loan size 2 x savings balance	None	None
Max 2 x savings balance+£300; max loan size £5,000 (US$7,500) over 2 years	Inputs for agricultural production in kind: range from seed to carts, ploughs etc. Max term 5 years	'Ordinary' loan max. 1m. sucres (US$400) over 15 months. Other types of loan available
1% dividend in 1995 -2%	n/a	n/a
12% 9	0 approx -10	52 (note 2) approx. 27
Credit Union as a whole defined by 'common bond' of residence: financial services provided to individuals	Village level groups administer credit; AATG provides training. Group level responsibility for repayment	Indigenous community committee structures and credit delegate represent community interests with CCC.

2 52% calculated as an annual percentage rate; 43% calculated on the declining balance basis

Table 6.2 Performance indicators of all Case Study Schemes in 1995
(All figures in US$)

Indicator	URAC Mexico	SUNGI Pakistan	Ladywood UK	AATG The Gambia	CCC Ecuador
No of savings accounts/members	4591	1260	270	---	---
No. of current borrowers/loans	1285 loans	137 borrowers	83 borrowers	Approx. 11,000 households have had access to loans	941 borrowers
Volume of savings	315,000	15,346	52,500	n/a	n/a
Volume of loans	113,485	21,545	55,500	107,100	375,741
% of users\members who are female	not available	61%	not available	60% (1)	Approx. 40%
Average savings balance	69	12	194	n/a	n/a
Average loan size	88	157	668	177(2)	350
Average loan size as % of GDP per capita (1993)	2	36	4	51	33
Repayment rates: • current on time repayment rate	95	100			
• % of loan volume ever taken and repaid				75	82
Arrears rate	4%		10%		8 %

1 indicates number of women members of village development groups having access to credit in one area with 140 villages rather than number of women actually taking loans. However, coverage within the group for seasonal loans was 70% upwards.
2 estimate

6.2 Union Regional de Apoyo Campesino (URAC), Mexico

6.2.1 Background

The Union Regional de Apoyo Campesino (URAC) is based in Tequisquiapan in the Mexican state of Queretaro. It was started in 1989 by Union de Esfuerzos para el Campo, (UDEC), a four-person NGO which began working around Tequisquiapan in 1984. URAC has a broad vision of building an alternative peasant economy in the region by encouraging the production of goods which *campesinos* (peasants) consume and the consumption of what the peasant union produces. Much of the work involves training village-based volunteer workers, and encouraging the organisational capacity of *campesinos* in the region. It is clear about its identity as a peasant organisation, rather than a savings and credit scheme, although the backbone of the work is currently the provision of financial services.

Mexico underwent radical economic reforms following the 1982 debt crisis. Low inflation, high capital in-flows from outside the country, and moderate economic growth masked a growing divide between rich and poor. This divide was expressed through a peasant uprising in the Southern state of Chiapas in January 1994. A series of events, including the assassination of the ruling party's presidential candidate, caused investor confidence to decline. This resulted in a new economic crisis in late 1994 when investors began to withdraw funds from short-term bonds and precipitated a run on the government's reserves of foreign exchange. Since then rescue packages have been organised by the IMF and World Bank to maintain Mexico's debt repayment obligations and secure the banking system. These efforts have not prevented inflation rates in the region of 50 per cent and similarly high interest rates. These in turn have resulted in defaults by middle-class borrowers on mortgages, car loans, and credit cards.

The four municipalities around Tequisquiapan in which URAC works have seen significant social and economic change in recent years. Rapid industrialisation in nearby towns had improved employment opportunities in the area although wages were poor, but these industries have suffered in the recent economic crisis. Agricultural employment is still provided on local estates and large farms, while some households have land-use rights under the terms of the land reforms of the 1930s, and others cultivate their own small plots. Male out-migration is high, both on a short-term basis to nearby towns and for longer-term work in the US. Remittances are therefore a major source of income.

6.2.2 Design

URAC is active in three main areas: financial services, agricultural and livestock production, and a programme to supply basic goods. The programme puts strong emphasis on organisation building and encouraging the involvement of members in monthly meetings at village level. The programme had some 5,000 members in 27 villages in 1995. There has been constant and steady growth, with a 60 per cent increase in membership between 1993 and 1996, reflecting the popularity of the programme in the villages in which it operates.

With its philosophy of self-sufficiency, URAC started with a savings-based approach. Members pay a membership fee and can save as much or as little as they wish. Members are organised into groups of between 20 and 70 people, and there may be two or three groups within a village. There is a monthly village meeting to give an update on the position of each group, including overdue loan instalments; information about the basic goods supply; news about URAC and about events in the region; followed by discussion of a broader issue, often a national or international theme, as well as technical discussions about agricultural production.

The function of the smaller groups is for saving. There is one cashier per group whose task it is to collect the savings and take them to the URAC office on a weekly basis. The savings facility is subject to a minimum deposit of 1 peso (US$0.15 in March 1996). The cashier decides when during the week she is willing to accept deposits, and the fact that this facility is available within the village makes it very convenient: members have been known to move between groups on the basis of the efficiency of the group's cashier. Withdrawals can be made on demand, but require more effort as they can only be made at the URAC office or mobile unit. However, the facility is well-used, and there is constant activity at the URAC office. Although this is not encouraged by staff, members sometimes ask the cashier to make with-drawals for them.

The savings facilities have also been adapted to suit local needs over time. URAC's 'optional' savings accounts are an interesting example of this. Members faced particularly high expenditures around periods of childbirth and school leaving. (It is customary for parties to take place in school and at home to celebrate school leaving. In almost every household there is a celebratory lunch involving the extended family.) The optional savings accounts were designed to meet these needs. Savings are regular but with-drawals can only be made three times a year when school semesters end, or at the time a baby is due. URAC has also established children's savings schemes. Children's groups are subsidiary to the adult ones and use the same cashiers.

Loan sizes are linked to savings balances. There is a requirement that 20 per cent of the loan is on deposit, which allows loans of five times the savings balance to be taken, up to a maximum for normal loans of N$700 (US$100; exchange rate N$6.6 = US$1 in March 1996). There is no restriction on what these loans can be used for. Quick-access loans in emergencies are also available under certain circumstances. Additional criteria for loan eligibility are attendance at meetings (a member must have attended the last three monthly meetings) and savings record (members must save at least N$1 per week).

A range of loan facilities are available, the main one being 'normal' loans described above; these are repayable over seven months. Loans for housing up to N$900 and 'responsible' loans of N$1000 are also available, on condition that members have demonstrated their ability to repay a normal loan and have 25 per cent of the loan amount in their savings account. A 'family' loan of up to N$4,000 for investment in a micro-enterprise requires applications to be made directly to URAC's Board. This loan also requires physical collateral or guarantees for half the value of the loan from other members. A further range of small-scale loans has recently been introduced for homestead production of small livestock and vegetables. These loans are administered through the savings and credit programme, partly because URAC finds them easier to monitor than loans issued through the agricultural production programme.

The group-based mechanism operates fairly loosely in terms of peer monitoring. Loan applications have to be endorsed by other members of the group (a group can in practice have up to 70 members) but this endorsement does not require that they take responsibility for repaying the loan in the event of default. However, if a member defaults, the group is denied access to further loans; individual defaulters lose access to their savings, which are used as collateral. Repayments are not made in public at group meetings but are taken by the individual borrower to URAC's office or to the mobile unit.

The groups are not the only way in which members participate in the Union. For example, group cashiers are involved in monthly decision-making meetings with URAC. They were involved in the recent decisions to tighten up the repayment policy and to allow loan instalments to be made in the villages as well as at head office.

Interest rates on savings and loans facilities differ depending on the service. In March 1996 the rate on 'normal' savings was 18 per cent per annum and on 'normal' loans was 30 per cent p.a. With inflation at rates of 50 per cent and above in Mexico since the peso crisis at the end of 1994, both savings and loan rates have been negative in real terms (see section 3.7 for an explanation of nominal and real interest rates). However, these interest rates were set by URAC before inflation rose so sharply and were initially highly positive in real terms. Now that inflation has again declined, URAC's real saving and borrowing rates are positive once more.

The project employs four full-time development workers (*promotores*) who undertake the main work of mobilisation at community level. They are assisted in this by two technicians — one agronomist and one vet (volunteer). Additionally, the URAC office has two clerical staff dedicated to the savings and credit programme and is open five days a week for members to transact their business. A mobile unit staffed by the development workers is open twice a week in Cadayreta, the part of the region furthest from Tequisquiapan. But the scheme depends heavily on the work of the group cashiers. Their role is to collect weekly savings and take them to the URAC office at least once a week, as well as to represent their groups in URAC meetings. In 1995 an incentive system was introduced to motivate the cashiers. It consisted of a points system for accurate record-keeping, with the points redeemable through the basic goods supply programme or as savings instalments or loan repayments. Performance has improved dramatically. Loan disbursement is carried out from the URAC office and until recently repayments could only be made at the office or mobile unit. Now, the development workers also collect loan instalments at the monthly village meeting, which reduces transport costs for borrowers.

Interlinked with the savings and credit scheme is the basic goods supply scheme which members qualify to use if they attend meetings and save regularly. Through a volunteer from the village, orders are placed fortnightly from a printed list of about 300 items and delivered to the village. Payment is made after two weeks at the time of making the next order. If an individual fails to pay on time the whole group is disqualified from using the facility.

6.2.3 Financial performance and sustainability

URAC collects a wide range of financial information which can be used to calculate either arrears, default rates or both, and reported a healthy repayment rate of 95 per cent in March 1996. Arrears are defined as loans for which full repayment has not been received seven days after the final due date. The number of loans in arrears has fallen consistently over the three years to 1995, as has the total volume outstanding. Arrears in 1995 represented some 14 per cent of the level of 1995 loan disbursement. The relationship between the arrears and defaults is especially interesting. The proportion of loans in arrears which eventually became defaults (defined as loans due for repayment in a particular year which are still not paid) rose from 8 per cent in 1994 to 27 per cent in 1995. This suggests that recent macro-economic contraction beginning in late 1994 has had a knock-on effect on URAC's loan performance by making repayment more difficult for members. Loan numbers declined in 1995, especially loans for housing construction; savings deposits remained steady in nominal terms, but this represented a fall in real terms.

From the start, URAC's philosophy has been one of self-sufficiency. This led to initial emphasis on savings mobilisation, and the core loan fund has never been dependent on donor capital, although loans in the separate agricultural production fund (not part of URAC's savings and credit component) have utilised donor money. As the calculations shown in Chapter 4 demonstrated, URAC reported a financial sustainability index of 47 per cent and a break-even interest rate of 76 per cent. This suggests that URAC is half-way towards achieving financial self-sustainability in its microfinance operations. The questions arising for URAC is how it might move towards full financial sustainability, and what the implications of this might be for the form and sustainability of the organisation.

As was pointed out in Chapter 4, one of the main elements of URAC's operating costs is the salaries of the four development workers. At present these workers are essential to the integrity of URAC's operations. In organisational terms, the challenge for URAC is therefore to find a strategy which enables costs to be covered without undermining this integrity.

6.2.4 Impact assessment

To understand the relevance and usefulness of the work of URAC, one of the 27 communities where the Union works was selected. The criteria for its selection included the programme having been in operation for at least three years, its being a village of average size, and one where URAC felt confident about the work it had done there. The focus of the research carried out was the savings programme.

The village of La Laja is adjacent to a deer-hunting ground, and includes a large working commercial dairy farm (*hacienda*). *Campesinos* cultivate land in privately owned smallholdings and use communal lands for grazing. However, there is extensive migration out of the area to find work. La Laja lies on the main road between Tequisquiapan and Queretaro. According to URAC, the village is not ethnically differentiated. All the inhabitants are *mestizo* by race and most are Roman Catholics. Most of the residents support the ruling Partido Revolucionario Institucional (PRI).

There are four URAC groups in the village, two each for adults and children with each of the two cashiers working for one adult and one children's group. Given the large size of the groups, up to 70 members, it was decided that the study would select a sample of households from just one group. Group membership involved more than one member of the same household, with 39 members covering a total of 26 households.

A wealth ranking exercise[1] offered insights into perceptions of what it meant to be relatively wealthy or relatively poor in La Laja. Respondents placed households into three categories: the wealthiest were referred to as those who *'tienen el modo'* (translated as 'those who have got it'); the middle group *'los amolados'* (the ground-down) and the poorest group *'los fregados'* (literally, the buggered). Indicators they used included:

- size of house, its condition, kitchen equipment (most importantly whether gas or wood was used for cooking) and bathroom;

- regularity of income and whether this is in the form of remittances from the USA;

- family size and ratio of workers to dependents.

Of the 19 respondents only one was male, a boy of 13; and in this case, most of the answers were provided by his mother. The main sources of income were remittances from male family members temporarily working in the USA; male workers in the construction industry (skilled and unskilled); and agricultural production (male and female), whether as paid workers on the local *hacienda* or as crop producers in their own right. Women were involved in petty trade, including the buying and selling of snacks and cheap jewellery in the village, small-scale food preparation, and domestic employment. One other woman traded on behalf of a company as an *abonero*, collecting payment instalments towards purchase of consumer durables selected from a catalogue.

The incomes of people in La Laja have been squeezed drastically by reduced opportunities for industrial employment (an estimated drop of 35-40 per cent between 1994 and 1996: Alfonso Castillo, personal communication) and escalating prices, especially for health care and education. In early 1996 the national inflation rate was running at approximately 50 per cent.

The URAC services have helped members to survive in times of difficulty and cope with unemployment following the 1994 crisis. Members used URAC to maintain economic security, despite savings deposits losing purchasing power through the operation of a negative real rate of interest. Its savings and loans components offer ways of saving that work out cheaper than alternatives such as *abonero* and less embarrassing than borrowing from relatives.

Most of the households operate more than one savings account. Often

---

1 The wealth-ranking and semi-structured interviewing in La Laja was carried out by Martha Romero.

women have accounts for themselves and for each of their children to which they contribute regularly. Most save weekly, although the amount may vary. Savings have been withdrawn for medical expenditure (including urgent treatment), survival in hard times (including sporadic unemployment), utility bills, raw materials for making household adornments, consumer durables (fridge, cupboard), clothes, shoes, school fees, and registration of a truck. Of those currently saving, half have taken loans for purposes such as house building and repair, school fees and uniforms, consumer durables (refrigerators), organisation of festivals (each year two villagers have to take this role), on-lending to non-members (including relatives outside the village), truck repairs, and credit instalments. Because the biggest category of loans are those for which no purpose needs to be specified, this data on loan use is likely to be reasonably reliable.

The advantages of the URAC services referred to by members included not having to save a fixed amount weekly (unlike ROSCAs); easy access to loans ,with minimal regulations and red tape; easy access to savings (including for urgent requirements); and the fact that individuals can safeguard cash without informing other household members.

Members adapt their use of the services to their preferences. Thus some people like to save and withdraw but would never consider borrowing; others take loans because they like the additional incentive to keep up payments. People who are very indebted cannot normally save and are thus unable to join the scheme; heavily indebted people who are already members become inactive. One respondent, a non-member, had previously saved in a co-operative bank (*caja*). However, faced with a serious illness in the family, she has had to live on withdrawn savings and has been unable to make new deposits.

It is important to understand how individuals make use of several financial services simultaneously; in particular how they borrow or withdraw from one source in order to meet commitments to another. One household reported paying school fees under a credit arrangement with monthly instalments. If these instalments are paid late, they increase by 10 per cent. A loan from URAC was used to ensure payments did not fall behind. Credit taken from local shops for groceries (a regular weekly practice for many members) was repaid from URAC savings. Half of the members interviewed had been actively involved in *tandas* (ROSCAs). In La Laja, one *tanda* was run by the *hacienda* owners; workers could opt to have 50 pesos per week deducted from their salary to be put into the group fund. Savings were also used for *tanda* instalments. In more than one case, members had also used co-operative banks based in Tequisquiapan for savings and loans. But this was common only among those who had relatively large amounts to save.

Members also used formal bank services on a one-off fee basis to receive remittances transferred from the USA.

6.2.5 Conclusions

URAC's savings and credit programme demonstrates the feasibility of operating a savings-based scheme from the outset. This savings base has limited the dependence of the programme on external funds to running costs alone.

URAC's flexible savings facilities are clearly appreciated by its members and used by them to support a wide range of livelihood needs, including food purchases, emergency health care, and insurance for periods of unemployment. In this way the services have demonstrated their usefulness and relevance to members and enabled them both to protect and improve their livelihoods.

The development of URAC's savings accounts to meet special needs, and those developed for children, demonstrates URAC's practice of continuously learning and adapting. URAC has achieved a high level of internally generated funds. Much of this success has been due to the hard work and commitment of the staff, whose salaries, in effect, have been funded from external sources.

6.3 SUNGI Development Foundation, Pakistan

6.3.1 Background

SUNGI Development Foundation (SUNGI) is an NGO formed in 1989 and operating in Hazara Division of the North-West Frontier Province (NWFP) of Pakistan. The Hazara Community Support Programme (HCSP), which SUNGI runs, grew out of a response to floods which hit the area in 1992. The HCSP began in 1994 and by December 1995 was working in 120 villages spread over four Districts. Apart from the small enterprise development component of the programme it includes work in health and sanitation, small-scale infrastructure, and forest management.

Compared to Pakistan as a whole, NWFP has fewer people below the income poverty line. While approximately half of all agricultural households in Pakistan rely on income from wage labour, in NWFP the proportion is less than one-third. Moreover, although agriculture is an important part of the regional economy, there is a relatively high reliance on non-agricultural income (Gazdar *et al*, 1996, p29).

The position of women in the society and economy of NWFP is particularly constrained in relation to enterprise development. Cultural norms limit their mobility outside of the homestead to engage in economic activities such as production and trade.

6.3.2 Design

SUNGI works with village organisations (VOs). These are set up for men and women separately. SUNGI will not work in a village unless there is both a men's and a women's organisation. The small enterprise development component is a savings and credit scheme. The VO elects a Credit Management Committee of at least four members. SUNGI works with this group to develop the credit policy of the village organisation, so detailed rules of operation vary from village to village. A membership fee is levied as a contribution to the VO. Of the five case studies, SUNGI's way of working most closely resembles the Grameen model, in which members are organised into 'solidarity groups' of five and offer guarantees in 'case of non-repayment by group members. However, while this is organisational policy, the operation of this mechanism varies significantly in practice between villages, as will be seen below.

Savings are compulsory for all members at 30 Rupees (about 90 US cents) per month. Members' savings are deposited by the village organisation into a bank account, in which they earn a 'profit and loss share'. (Islamic law prohibits interest being charged on loans or paid on deposits.) In theory savings are retrievable from this account, but policies guiding the terms and conditions of access had not been worked out with the VOs by the time of the case-study research.

Loans are available to individuals up to a limit of Rs5,000 (about US$150). All loans are subject to an annual service charge of 18 per cent in the context of an annual inflation rate of 10 per cent. The interest rate income is divided as follows: 14 per cent to SUNGI's loan fund, 2 per cent for SUNGI's operational costs, and 2 per cent for the Village Organisation.

All loans are intended for productive income-generating purposes and vary in term from six to 24 months. Repayment schedules are designed to reflect the income stream of the investment. Physical collateral is not required, but guarantees must be sought from other members of the five-member groups into which people are organised. The co-guarantors of the loan must keep a minimum of 15 per cent of the loan value in their savings accounts.

SUNGI's village-level workers are called Field Coordinators. It is the Coordinator's job to undertake a feasibility study to investigate whether the economic activity proposed is viable. The application for credit is submitted by the Credit Management Committee through the Field Coordinator to the SUNGI monthly management meeting, where a decision is made.

In one village, it was found that, due to the dynamic leadership of the village organisation by a local teacher, the operation of the scheme was largely conducted by him on a house-to-house basis, and those taking loans were not necessarily even aware of who the other four members who had signed their loan applications were.

6.3.3 Financial performance and sustainability

SUNGI started disbursing loans in 1995 and to date has not had any problems with repayment. It is difficult to discuss its performance so far given the small number of loans that have been made.

In particular it is too early to judge financial sustainability. Organisational sustainability for NGOs working in this area may require a more enabling legal framework, especially with regard to the collection of savings deposits.

6.3.4 Impact assessment

It is also too early to attempt detailed investigations of the role loans have played in relation to members' livelihoods. The case study therefore concentrated on understanding the way in which SUNGI's model was working out in practice: the relationship of the scheme to other informal financial services; and the way in which different groups within the community were participating in it. The experiences of women in obtaining and using loans were of particular interest given the system of *purdah* (female seclusion) predominant in the area.

The case study was confined to two villages selected by SUNGI. Livelihood activities in this part of NWFP include manual work (male) on the railways; livestock-rearing and dairying (female and male); and wheat cultivation (male). Casual work for men is available in the enormous Jepsum quarry adjacent to one of the villages.

In Barilla, a large village consisting of a number of separate hamlets, with a total population of 10,000, the male VO had existed prior to involvement with SUNGI. It started in 1991 in one hamlet to carry out infrastructural work and repairs, and by 1995 had 119 members across the village as a whole. The driving force behind this organisation is a local teacher. The executive council of 15 members is selected rather than elected, with some based outside the area; two members of the Credit Management Committee were based in Islamabad for most of the week. The Women's Organisation is also led by a local teacher. Its formation is more recent but its success in mobilising savings has already drawn the attention of other (larger) financial services providers. One of these is the First Women's Bank of Pakistan, which has visited Barilla to study SUNGI's methods. In the other village, Karach, the male VO had been formed in 1994 as a result of SUNGI's work and its parallel women's organisation started soon afterwards.

A total of 17 semi-structured interviews were carried out, with male and female members, some of whom had already taken loans, and with two non-members. A relatively high proportion of those interviewed had access to regular salaries or were relatively well-remunerated from self-employment.

Only one household relied on income from agriculture, and the majority had multiple income sources. The researchers were immediately conscious of obvious wealth differences on entering the villages; and the sensitivity about wealth and poverty made a wealth-ranking exercise inappropriate. As a result, respondents could not be selected to represent all social ranks and wealth groups. However, because of the small number of loans, it was possible to meet a large proportion of borrowers.

On the savings side all members were making the minimum compulsory contribution of Rs30 per month. However, understanding of the profit share and withdrawal options was confused. The SUNGI system operates savings as a relatively inflexible component. It is one thing to have to save but quite another to have to save a fixed amount and not to have automatic withdrawal rights. The fact that none of the respondents saved more than the required Rs30 per month suggests that for most of them at least the compulsory savings are part of the price they have to pay for their loans.

Sources of informal finance in Barilla and Karach included loans from neighbours and ROSCAs known locally as *kamitis*. Loans from neighbours were considered very pressurising because of the degree of shame involved if the loans were not repaid on time. There was very little evidence of high-interest private informal lending, and only one woman was reported to be an interest-charging money lender in Barilla. (VO leaders attached importance to not charging interest as it was forbidden in Islam.)

Kamitis were used in general by better-off respondents and were more common in the wealthiest part of Barilla. The *kamitis* in Barilla involved groups of between 9 and 25 people and equal monthly instalments ranging from Rs30 to Rs2000 per month and pay-offs of Rs300 to Rs32,000. Some households were involved simultaneously in more than one *kamiti*.

The uses to which *kamiti* pay-outs were put included house building, deposit into a formal-bank savings account, payment for sons in higher education, and marriage of daughters. None of these purposes would have qualified for a loan under the SUNGI scheme as none of them fell into the five possible categories of productive loan. This indicates that for households involved in *kamitis* the SUNGI intervention is to an extent complementary.

The stated purpose for loans taken by interviewees included livestock rearing and small businesses such as shops, sewing, and rope making. However, without fairly expensive monitoring and follow-up systems on SUNGI's part, which do not currently exist because responsibility is taken by the VO's credit management committee, there can be no assurance that loans are being used for the purposes stated. While it did appear that loans were being used for income augmentation rather than 'protection' alone, it was also clear that those on the lowest incomes tended not to take part. The situation of two non-members reinforces this view. They were unable to make the necessary savings to join the scheme, and were dependent on private loans to cover their needs or were paying-off earlier loans.

Almost all of those interviewed were paying their instalments on time. This is probably due, in Barilla at least, to the personal involvement of the organisation's office-holders in repayment enforcement. Thus the operation of the model in practice differs significantly between the villages.

Within the household, loans are managed in different ways. Intra-household loan management and control was discussed with six borrowers — five women and one man. Below, the experiences of three women borrowers are given, to illustrate terms of control of the asset purchased and associated tensions within the households.

The first woman, who is 22 years old, and lives in Barilla village with her husband and three small children, described their main sources of cash income as the clerical salary her husband earns (Rs2000 per month) and her own occasional embroidery (Rs20-40 per month). Her husband went to market to purchase the two goats she bought with her loan of Rs4500. She carries out most of the tasks associated with the goats' upkeep and her husband provides loan repayment instalments from his salary. Sometimes there are arguments with her husband when she needs cash. The goats themselves do not provide an income stream; in fact, one of them died. However, the remaining one is a source of milk for the children, and she hopes to earn some cash when she sells the animal. Although she very much values the savings component of the women's organisation's work, she has had to oppose her brothers who advised her to deposit money in the bank to gain more interest.

Another woman borrower, much better-off and living with her husband and three salaried sons, was the mother of one of the leading members of the Barilla village organisation. Her monthly income is over Rs4000. She received Rs5000 for rope-making (for string cots) and travelled to Faisalabad herself to purchase the raw material. The income she makes, which was not revealed, is controlled by her alone. She attends monthly meetings regularly and plans to apply for a loan for a bigger business.

A third woman, 35 years old and an office-holder in the Karach women's organisation, took a two-year loan of Rs5000 to start a shop. She lives with her five children. Her husband is employed as a daily labourer in Islamabad. He brings back Rs1300-1500 per month and she earns Rs320 per month for stitching clothes. Once her brothers-in-law came to know about her loan, they took over the management of the shop, and gave her Rs150-200 per month income (her loan instalments are Rs250 per month). She has been subjected to violence by her husband who used to beat her during arguments about money, even before she took out the loan. Recently, although pregnant, she says she was badly beaten as her husband wrongly thought she had received a high per diem for taking part in a SUNGI training exercise. Once this loan is repaid she plans to take another loan for livestock rearing. She is more confident that she will be allowed to manage the work involved herself.

6.3.5 Conclusions

SUNGI's small enterprise development programme started in 1994. Using a model based on micro-enterprise loans, compulsory savings, and small lending groups, with guarantees on loans provided by other members within the group, SUNGI's approach resembles that of the Grameen Bank.

Short visits of a few days to each of two villages revealed differences in the ways VOs disbursed loans and collected savings. Early indications suggested that in those villages repayments were being made on time. In one case actual repayment enforcement was carried out by VO office-holders rather than the members of the small borrowing groups.

The few women borrowers interviewed reported diverse experiences. While in one case, the borrower retained control over the whole small enterprise (including purchasing inputs from Faisalabad), in another, the enterprise was taken over by male relatives.

6.4 Ladywood Credit Union, UK

6.4.1 Background

Ladywood is an inner-city area of Birmingham, UK. The Ladywood Project has set up a range of initiatives, including a drop-in centre for parents and small children, a women's group, a domestic violence forum, and a furniture exchange, where poor families can obtain second-hand donated furniture. The Project operates from a Community and Health Centre. It was workers on the Ladywood Project who began the Ladywood Credit Union (LCU) in 1987 with the support of the Birmingham Credit Union Development Agency. Registered unemployment in the area is 29 per cent for men and 20 per cent for women, compared with 10 and 5 per cent respectively in the UK as a whole (1991, Census of Population). The result is a high dependence on state welfare benefits. Earlier experience of the Ladywood Project had revealed the high extent of indebtedness and personal financial difficulties in the area.

LCU is not a commercial organisation and its activities are closely defined by the restrictive framework of the 1979 UK Credit Union Act. This requires that members must have a 'common bond' defined by either workplace, location or faith. Workplace or employee credit unions are quite distinct from community credit unions, as members of the former have regular incomes and assets can therefore be built up rapidly. However, the maximum savings that an individual can hold in a credit union is £5000. Savings are held in the form of shares and the maximum dividend payment allowed on them, by law, is 8 per cent p.a.

As part of the Ladywood Project, the role of LCU goes beyond financial service provision, although many members use it solely for that purpose. Activist members, including the former and current development workers, and the staff of the Ladywood Project, see its role as more broadly supportive of members in financial difficulties.

The informal and flexible way of working which has been developed at LCU, together with a friendly and open attitude towards new members, makes it more than just a service provider. Also the history of the LCU, which has relied on voluntary labour, sharing office space with the Ladywood Project, and calling on members to share skills which would have been pro-hibitively expensive on the market (such as book-keeping and accountancy), distinguishes it from commercial providers of financial services. Its core members also explicitly set out to provide (through both voluntary work and financial security) a means of building self-esteem, of being in control of one's own life, of being valued and able to contribute and develop personal skills[2].

6.4.2 Design

The LCU is staffed by one full-time development worker who has been funded by Birmingham City Council since 1991, and a number of volunteers who are either from the community or are associated with the Ladywood Project in some way. Volunteers are vital to the project and LCU could not survive if it had to pay them salaries. LCU operates through a series of committees which are part of the structure prescribed by law. These com-mittees involve community members as well as staff of the project. Their role is to monitor each other. There is a Board of Directors, a Loans Committee, a

2 Much of this analysis of the impact of LCU's work was written by (and almost all the semi-structured interviewing was carried out by) Helen Derbyshire.

Credit Control Committee, and a Supervisory Committee which carries out regular checks on the operation of the other committees.

LCU offers a voluntary savings facility. Members can deposit as little as they like. Withdrawals of up to £10 (about US$17) can be made at the main office (open four afternoons a week) or at one of the various satellite collection points which operate on a part-time basis. Larger amounts may take longer, but for those who suffer mobility problems, these rules are implemented very flexibly. LCU has only been able to pay a dividend on savings for the first time in 1995 at a rate of 1 per cent. Up to this point, it had used its income from loan interest to build reserves against bad debt.

Members of LCU conduct their activities entirely independently. Security for loans is provided by savings balances and the 'common bond' of local residence, rather than group collateral. While loan size can be a maximum of twice the savings balance plus £300, (US$500), subject to a legally prescribed ceiling, a crucial component of judging applications is examining past savings deposits and attempting to set the loan instalments to levels just below the amount, and at the intervals at which, the borrower usually saves. This is done in order to try and ensure that savings balances continue to rise. Quick-access loans in emergencies are also available.

Interest rates on loans stand at 12 per cent p.a, resulting in a real rate of around 9 per cent. However, credit of the type LCU offers to its members (much of which is used for consumption) would only be available at rates of interest of at least 20 per cent from the formal sector in the UK. LCU members would also face many other barriers in trying to obtain such loans.

Members automatically qualify for life insurance cover, which LCU purchases in bulk via the Association of British Credit Unions. This would pay off any outstanding loans and provide twice the value of savings to a previously named beneficiary in the event of death.

LCU is involved in two important innovations. The first is the Junior Savers Scheme. Three of the four satellite collection points are in schools, and there are now 400 child members, some of whom get involved in keeping computerised records for the scheme.

LCU has also been involved in a scheme run by Birmingham Credit Union Development Agency to connect up three inner-city credit unions by using modem links between computers, enabling members to use the offices of any of the three to undertake transactions. In addition, LCU took part in research to establish the business potential for a bill-paying service. Bills for utilities (gas, electricity, water) are major expenses for poor people. Not only do they often find it difficult to organise their payments on a regular basis but they also incur high transport costs and fees in paying bills. The business plan suggests that a service could be provided more cheaply than the one the Post

Office currently provides, and that it would be commercially viable in the long run. The capital funding for the project has not yet been raised.

6.4.3 Financial performance and sustainability

Ladywood Credit Union has experienced some difficulties with the timing of repayments. In about one-third to one-half of all loans there are gaps of three weeks or more in repayment instalments, which are usually weekly. However, part of Ladywood's service is that it investigates non-payers and is flexible in repayment schedules. Such a situation is only possible because of the small number of members, and the close supervision available. Some 58 per cent of borrowers can be in arrears at any one time but at present serious default cases run at approximately 10 per cent of the loan fund and involve some 25 per cent of those with loans outstanding. This suggests that it is those with small loans who find it difficult to repay, and this is likely to be explained by the earlier observation that the scheme also has members who have salaries and take out loans for relatively large consumer items such as cars. This profile of membership and lending, in which better-off members are able to take larger loans which involve lower risks for LCU, suggests that to some extent these users are helping to ensure the availability of LCU's services to its poorer members.

LCU's accounts show a healthy situation in which profits were made in the second half of 1995. However, this calculation does not include staff costs. At present the work is carried out by volunteers and a full-time development worker whose salary is paid by Birmingham City Council. Office space is free as part of the wider Ladywood Project. A sustainability index calculated on the basis of costing all inputs would probably indicate that Ladywood was not financially sustainable.

However, LCU has demonstrated an ability to mobilise the voluntary work and other inputs required to sustain the union, and UK credit union law does not allow it to operate at a financial loss. Indeed, the voluntary work of the staff and their commitment are integral to the project in supporting an element of social interaction which is central to the project's way of working. This demonstrates the limitations of evaluating financial sustainability on the basis of a narrow financial calculation, especially in cases where it is possible to sustain voluntary inputs in the long term.

6.4.4 Impact assessment

In order to understand the role LCU plays for its members, semi-structured interviews were carried out with 19 individuals. The respondents were selected by the current and former LCU development workers to reflect the range of members' socioeconomic backgrounds in terms of income, race, gender, age, and location. It was emphasised that interviews with poorer members and ex-members were of particular interest.

Overall, members could be divided into two groups:

- Those living on government benefits and/or very low employment income, often single parents, who used the Credit Union to control domestic finances. If they took loans, these members would tend to use them to pay domestic bills, cover the costs associated with Christmas or other festivals, and the purchase and repair of items of household equipment such as cookers and washing machines.

- People with more regular incomes, including professionals employed in the Ladywood Project, for whom the main attraction was low-cost loans for larger items such as holidays, weddings, and cars.

However, the credit union membership did not generally include the very poorest Ladywood residents, i.e. people living in debt. Kempson, in a wider study of those excluded from the banking system in the UK (HMSO report, 1994), classifies credit unions as 'mid-market'. As Kempson explains, credit-union members need to save in order to access loans. Most people without current accounts in high-street banks are not in a position to build up savings. In a separate study among poor people of Bangladeshi, Pakistani and Carribean origin in the UK, Herbert and Kempson (1996) found that, despite differences in credit use between these groups, all of them relied either on informal rotating savings and credit associations or friends, relatives, and the private informal sector (including pawn-brokers and foreign exchange agents) rather than credit unions.

The interviews demonstrated that some members see LCU as a preventive measure to keep themselves out of a downward spiral of indebtedness to private credit-companies. The savings facilities of LCU, like those of URAC, are extremely useful to such people. It is those who are already heavily indebted who find it hard to manage a regular savings commitment as any income is already committed to existing creditors.

In Ladywood indebtedness to private loan companies is common and mostly affects those people whose income is derived from benefits and various forms of casual labour. They borrow to meet consumption needs, such as clothes and household items, by obtaining them through mail-order catalogues or with high-interest loans taken from private credit-companies. A government-run Social Fund provides loans for items of essential domestic expenditure, such as cookers and beds, with repayments being deducted at source in fixed amounts from benefits. Private credit-company loans are provided in the form of vouchers for particular shops, or immediate unsecured cash loans to be repaid at very high rates of interest.

There are increasing numbers of private credit-companies offering cash loans and shopping vouchers to people living in Ladywood. Their services are advertised in local shops and through leafleting door-to-door. Credit-company agents, who are paid on a commission basis, visit people at home to provide loans and to collect repayments. Interest rates on loans are high: in most cases more than 50 per cent per annum. The credit-companies are providing a service which is extremely widely known and widely used, and to which, for those not in a position to save, there is often no alternative.

Respondents described how the private credit-companies often tried to persuade people to take on more loans, even when they knew they were already heavily indebted. They therefore saw the purpose of the credit union as useful for the thrifty, preventing indebtedness through savings, and providing a means of building security against uneven cash needs. One of the clear advantages of the private credit-companies was the immediate nature of their loans, given without collateral. There is thus a philosophical difference between the credit union and the private loan-companies. While the former promote an ethic of thrift, providing people with a means of being in control of their own finances, and living within their income, the latter tempt people to spend, live beyond their means, and count the cost tomorrow.

LCU users who live on benefits or very low incomes tend to save in irregular small amounts. They reported using loans to help to pay for items such as TV licences, utility bills, and life insurance. Such members felt they could not use banks due to embarrassment at the small amounts they deposited. They also make extensive use of the other sources of credit described above. Some who had tried to save in the credit union, found themselves unable to keep up with their initial expectations of their own savings capacity. Those people on benefits who use the credit union are very positive about it, stressing in particular the understanding approach of staff, the flexibility, the chance it provides to save in small amounts, the low rate of interest on loans, and the greater sense of control it offers them in difficult circumstances.

The majority of LCU members fall into the second category: they are people who have a regular income, including some professionals. All of these people have bank or building-society accounts into which their salaries are paid, and make contributions to LCU by means of automatic transfers. A minority of people in this category save with a building society as well as with LCU, as a way of diversifying assets. Some people in African-Caribbean communities combine LCU savings with revolving savings and loans ('partner' arrangements). One of the advantages of such arrangements is the discipline in savings required which is enforced through strong social sanctions. But for those who find it impossible to meet the fixed weekly commitment, LCU offers a flexible alternative.

6.4.5 Conclusions

The case of LCU illustrates a number of points of relevance to the themes of this book. First, the difficulties of reaching those who are already highly indebted and unable to make even small but regular savings which might eventually qualify them for a loan. Second, the combination of a financial service with a strong social support structure which encourages people to take control of their finances. Third, the role that other members of the local community can and do make in providing the service. These better-off people contribute by investing their capital and hence providing the funds for on-lending, taking and repaying loans so providing LCU an income. Some can also be counted among the volunteers from all income groups who give their time to assist in the running of the credit union.

6.5 ACTIONAID in The Gambia

6.5.1 Background

ACTIONAID has been working in the small West African state of The Gambia since 1981. With a population of approximately 1 million, The Gambia has a GDP per capita of US$350 (1993). The bulk of the population is rural and dependent on agriculture. There is a single rainy season and only limited irrigation facilities along the Gambia river, and food security is a major concern. Agricultural development activities have always been central to the ACTIONAID The Gambia (AATG) programme. AATG works in over one-sixth of the villages of The Gambia (591 villages in all). It is largely funded through child sponsorship in the UK, and in the early 1980s operated by giving grants to individuals and organisations. Many grants were given in kind in the form of seasonal inputs of seed and fertiliser as well as agricultural implements, such as ploughs, sinehoes, and weeders. By 1987, this was changed to a 'half grant: half credit' approach in which the credit repayments were used to finance further input supply. This approach moved to a 'full credit' system in which the full value of the credit was repaid; and since 1992 the strategy has been to locate this credit system within the village organisations and groups with which AATG works.

These Village Development Groups (VDGs) have in many cases grown out of existing village institutions, including local savings and credit groups (*kafos* and *osusus*). AATG disburses interest-free loans to the VDG. The VDG allocates loans among members and may charge interest to members if it wishes. Repaid credit is kept in a Trust Account for each particular village. Since 1992, if the original loan capital has been repaid in full, AATG has made it available once more to the VDG to use for its own purposes ('recycling'). This can include on-lending to individuals. Thus AATG is attempting to use financial capital to build the resource bases of existing village institutions.

6.5.2 Design

AATG has done little to stimulate saving by groups. However, groups are helped to open bank accounts in up-country branches of commercial banks into which they deposit membership fees. When AATG returns their Trust Account funds to them, this is done by a transfer to their bank account.

Loans available from AATG have generally been provided in kind. They have covered seasonal inputs, such as seeds and fertiliser, which are repayable within a year; medium-term loans for agricultural implements, such as seeders and sinehoes, for between one and three years; and long-term loans of animal carts and oxen. Repayments are usually scheduled annually on the anniversary of the loan.

The AATG fieldworker receives applications from the group for loans, and these are passed on to the project's credit committees for vetting against a range of criteria, including whether the community has overdue loans. If it has, it should receive no further loans. This rule was introduced in 1992 after loans had been issued to many communities and not repaid. However, repayment is often related to the strength and attitude of the village group, some groups being better organised and more interested in development activities than others. The 'recycling' of money to communities has acted as an incentive for some groups to pay-off outstanding loans in order to gain access to their Trust Funds. Others believe that what they have received should be treated as a grant, a clear hangover from AATG's past programming approach.

AATG undertakes a range of activities including work in education and health. It has also worked with the groups and village organisations to expand their organisational and management skills. Training is provided to group executive committees, which are encouraged to extend their membership to all households in the village. Many of the organisations are almost entirely composed of women. In its early days, AATG worked mainly with group enterprises and farms and, since women's groups were common, tended to work with them. However, the degree of women's representation currently varies from village to village. Some of the groups have only a very small number of male members.

AATG has never charged interest on loans. It takes the view that the loans are made to the village groups who can on-lend them with interest if they want to. However, in practice there is no evidence that this occurs for loans given directly by AATG. Where AATG has returned repaid loan funds to the group to utilise in their own way, evidence suggests that they are being lent out by the group at interest. These rates are difficult to calculate because the groups undertake a range of activities, such as purchase of food or seed which is stocked locally (very similar to the basic goods supply scheme in URAC), which may be offered in kind and repaid in cash. Groups tend to offer a range of terms on the type and nature of the loans.

6.5.3 Financial performance and sustainability

In AATG, the repayment rate of 75 per cent is calculated as a historical figure taking account of the whole period of the scheme; the 'on-time' repayment rate is likely to be lower. The method of calculation is related to the programme's policy of 'recycling' funds to the VDGs once they have repaid their loans. This shift of policy has improved recovery rates in a number of villages since villagers have realised that they can receive more resources if they put pressure on those who have not repaid. There is evidence that groups have seized assets from non-payers as a result.

AATG takes a very different approach to the issue of organisational and financial sustainability. It argues that it has never been and does not intend to be a microfinance institution. Rather its objective is to develop the institutional mechanisms that exist in the villages in which it works. Its change of strategy in 1992 from service delivery to institutional development underlines this approach. While it continues to offer credit to villagers, the way in which repayments are paid into Trust Funds for those villages means that the village is building its own capital fund through repaying. Against certain criteria of organisational development, the village is then allowed to apply for the return of those funds to be operated under its own management. This is an example of how this is now operating in one village:

> *The VDG in Demfaye Njaga has 58 women and five men, representing a total of 29 households. It is well-organised and operates by dividing into small cells within which D5 per month is collected. This money is deposited in the village safe and is used for emergencies. The village safe is not allowed to 'go dry'. If loans are needed for an emergency, a small number of members of the loans committee are able to decide and report to the next executive meeting. Emergency loans are interest-free if repaid quickly (within a month).*

> *The group has received D28,253 back from AATG ($2,500) via its group bank deposit account. It withdrew D8,000, of which D7,000 was given out to members as cash credit at 15 per cent interest over four months, to be repaid at the end of the dry season. D1000 was given out as loans for small business operations, which made D1280 profit.*
>
> *A further D11,000 was then withdrawn and distributed as cash loans, some of which were used to buy food, others for trading. There have been no problems with repayment so far. None of the loans are given directly to men because the women feel that they have no authority over them to ensure repayment.*
>
> *This group has also taken a loan from the Gambia Village Development Trust which was offered at a rate of interest of 18 per cent over one year. It was used for buying carts which were given as loans to men and for ram-fattening activities. The profit made on this loan was D570.*

AATG is now building on the experience of recycling funds by looking at how it can support the continued development of financial services through training and support. Not all village groups are as well-organised as the group in Demfaye Njaga, and some have had problems with repayment. AATG's approach is still being refined. Among the 591 villages in which AATG works, not all will want to run, or be capable of running, their own financial institution. Some VDGs may invest in development projects and not revolve the capital fund. Some are likely to be development organisations with financial resources at their disposal, rather than village banks.

6.5.4 Impact assessment

For the AATG case study semi-structured interviews were carried out with a sample of 42 individuals in eight villages. This was one part of a research initiative which included establishing information on coverage and other sources of credit. The individuals selected included men and women, those with short- and long-term loans, and non-borrowers.

Seasonal loans had been received by upwards of 70 per cent of VDG members. However, this had sometimes meant very small amounts of seed or fertiliser (such as a quarter of a bag of fertiliser) as the VDG would decide to distribute the inputs it received equally to all members. The extent of coverage of long-term loans for agricultural implements was much more varied, ranging from 5 to 67 per cent of VDG members. The differences in coverage between villages often reflected the fact that villages which had not repaid had not been given further loans.

Five individuals interviewed reported non-repayment of more than one loan. This can be related to AATG's relatively 'soft' policy on loan repayment, especially prior to 1991. In three of these cases the village had received no new loans since 1991 as a result of this non-payment. In the remaining two cases further new loans had been received by the village in spite of the policy change.

Of the 30 respondents who summarised what a loan had meant to them, only one mentioned a negative impact. (The loan was for a donkey which had had to be sold following non-repayment due to a bad harvest.) The remaining 29 reported increased production, improved yield, more food, less need to borrow from elsewhere, and reduced length of the 'hungry season'. One respondent, the President of one of the VDGs, had taken three long-term, fixed-capital loans for a sinehoe, seeder, and cart, and claimed he was unable to repay any of them due to poor harvests. In this case, the use of social position to obtain a relatively high number of long-term loans was combined with non-repayment. (It is interesting to contrast this with the example of one village in the Casa Campesina Cayambe project (Ecuador), in which relatively wealthy office-holders took more loans than others, but repaid them; and with the Ladywood Credit Union in Birmingham which relies on larger loans taken out by relatively well-off people to generate income for the organisation from interest payments.)

The evidence suggested that seasonal working-capital loans had expanded the supply of relatively scarce inputs. Although yields have improved as a result of fertiliser use, it appeared the increases had not reduced the length of the hungry season and there was no evidence that they had enabled processes of accumulation and expansion of agricultural production to take place over subsequent seasons either.

The impression of researchers was that women borrowers and poorer borrowers were more likely to repay, but also that the poorest exclude themselves from larger loans, not wanting to jeopardise their access to future credit through gaining a reputation for being uncreditworthy. Indebtedness has increased in some of the AATG villages, however, partly because of the inter-annual variation in rainfall: most loans are agriculture-related and agricultural production is rainfall dependent. However, non-payment is also due to the 'soft' line on repayment taken by AATG. A tougher stance might have led to higher repayment but also to more self-exclusion by potential users.

Of the eight villages where the study took place, six had received recycled funds. The main use of these funds, which are allocated entirely by the VDG, has been to provide hungry season consumption loans, often through setting up small retail shops within the village. (This indicates a similar need to that addressed by URAC, for the convenient supply of basic consumer items.) There had been a limited supply of loans for consumption purposes previously, with capital available to groups only from pre-existing group savings. Because most *kafo* groups already have experience of providing small cash loans out of their own savings, the recycling of funds was taking advantage of an indigenous system, which was already working well. Loans made out of recycled funds carry relatively high interest rates, but also achieve high repayment rates. Recycled funds have also been used to provide agricultural implements, such as sinehoes and seeders, on credit to members.

The seasonal loans made by AATG and the consumption loans made out of group revolving funds have enabled many women to cope with immediate needs. However, assets received in women's names as long-term loans are owned and controlled by the male household head. In one group, women reported that men were habitual non-repayers and that they did not have the means to enforce repayment from men.Therefore they did not give loans to men.

AATG's main objective since 1992 has been the establishment of village institutions and it now sees credit as a means through which group org-anisation and management can be strengthened as well as provided with financial resources. The need for 100 per cent repayment before further loans are sanctioned, and the system of recycled funds, has introduced incentives for group cohesion and management which did not exist prior to 1992.

While earlier policies had resulted in poor loan repayment in many villages, there was no evidence that this had resulted in non-payment of *kafo* loans. This contrasts with the findings of research which suggests that 'soft' policies might 'contaminate' indigenous lending practices (Nagarajan, Meyer and Graham, 1995). In one village, Sinchu Tamsir, where the AATG scheme is not performing well in terms of loan repayments, indigenous group activities continue to be effective. Non-payment in the AATG system in this case had been a result of the abuse of the system by the village head, an option that was clearly not open to him in the indigenous system.

The apparent success of recycling funds raises questions about the necessity of the continued existence of the AATG credit work. An alternative approach would be to make capital grants into pre-existing group revolving funds (where such funds can be seen to be working well) to expand their capital base.

However, with declining profitability on marketed groundnuts, reduced remittances from urban migrants due to increasing unemployment, and the shrinkage in the tourist trade, rural livelihoods are under pressure. AATG's credit-cum-grants and the recycled funds make a small contribution to the capitalisation of village institutions and to the coping mechanisms of poor households. Seasonal loans in particular have enabled poor households to protect their livelihoods, through the use of otherwise inaccessible agricult-ural inputs which result in greater yields.

In some cases better-off households are able to use the capital to accumulate wealth without respecting the repayment requirements. There is insufficient evidence to judge whether this increases socio-economic differentiation. The recycling of repaid loans to village groups has meshed well with existing systems for group investment and allocation of loans. There is also no evidence to suggest that the soft line on repayment enforcement in the AATG credit scheme negatively influences the working of indigenous *kafos*. However, it is possible that this experience will complicate the efforts of other external agencies aiming at sustainable microfinance initiatives.

6.5.5 Conclusions

AATG is the largest operational NGO in The Gambia where it has been working since the early 1980s. Its size and history influence current performance both in terms of users' attitudes to the project as well as the organisational constraints in deciding and implementing major changes in policy and approach. Changes are often piloted with smaller numbers of villages before being extended as general policy. Such constraints mean that change takes time to agree, experiment with, and then implement throughout the agency. The understanding of fieldworkers and community members is key and it is often more difficult to communicate changes in policy during a programme than when starting up in new areas.

AATG has decided that its main aim is to build strong rural institutions rather than to become a sustainable financial intermediary itself. The shift to community-based management systems which was introduced in 1992 was brought about as a result of lessons learned from its own work and a desire to move its own practice forward. This major shift in policy has taken time to implement, but interesting results are beginning to show, with groups demonstrating their ability to manage recycled funds. The strength of local communities' existing skills in management of *osusus* and *kafos* have contributed to the success of this policy. In turn this indicates what can be learned from an exploration of indigenous systems of financial services.

6.6 Casa Campesina Cayambe, Ecuador

6.6.1 Background

Casa Campesina Cayambe (CCC) was set up by a Salesian priest in 1987 as an extension of work that Salesian fathers had been undertaking for several decades. It works with indigenous Quichua Indians in four parishes, 80km north of Quito, at an altitude of some 2,800 metres in the Andes.

The villages depend on agriculture and livestock. They farm land regained after the collapse of a co-operative system, which had taken over land from large estates after land reform legislation. The land-holdings of poorer households are typically as small as two hectares and necessitate seasonal migration of family members for agricultural labour or to the cities. Annual family incomes are approximately US$300 compared with a national per capita average of US$1200 (1993 figures). While literacy is high, at 87 per cent, child malnutrition is also high, at 50 per cent.

CCC's financial services are an example of NGO credit-provision in a closely defined geographical area. Loans were initially allocated through the Centros Infantiles Campesinos, the creches for children aged three to six. Loans were available to the children's parents, funds coming directly from Ayuda en Accion. At the same time, Foderuma (the government programme for which the charismatic CCC leader had worked as promoter) was allocating loans through village-level organisations. Foderuma loans were given in kind in the form of agricultural inputs. Foderuma was dissolved in 1994.

6.6.2 Design

The project operates in the three sectors of production, education, and health. The credit programme exists as part of the production programme but is not exclusively credit for production. There is no savings component. CCC does not operate a group mechanism of its own, rather it operates through the Quichua's indigenous system of Community Committees, which exist independently of CCC. The loan application must be approved by the Community Committee and be signed by the Credit Delegate and Community Directorate before being passed to the Inter-Community Credit Committee (CIC). This committee, which consists of a delegate from each of the villages, meets monthly. It approves applications for loans and decides on the allocation of credit between communities. The sanction of no further loans to the community is applied when an individual defaults. Continued non-payment results in legal proceedings being brought against the borrower by the CIC.

Credit is provided in a number of categories. 'Ordinary' credit is the main type of loan with a maximum amount of 1 million sucres (Approx. US$400 in 1995) which can be used for any purpose. This amount has been raised over the years as inflation has been high, but the project has attempted to retain this limit at a level which would ensure a degree of coverage for poorer members, and to correspond to the debt-carrying capacities of households. Other loans available are: 'special' loans in cases of illness or domestic emergency; loans for the installation of bathrooms — a total of 600 have been installed to date; credit for housing construction, involving a group of about ten people who apply together, and the provision of building materials in kind through a supplier; and credit for new productive activities — these are micro-enterprise ventures usually in fish production or cheese making in which the project also carries some of the risk of failure and provides a large degree of training and technical support. Further categories of credit available are for grassland and seed improvement.

CCC charges 52 per cent (APR) on ordinary loans or 43 per cent if calculated on the basis of declining balance. (APR is Annual Percentage Rate. For example, CCC charges 325,000 sucres for a loan of 1,000,000 which is repaid in five equal three-monthly instalments; 325,000 interest is therefore paid on an average loan balance of 500,000, representing 65 per cent over 15 months or 52 per cent over 12 months.) This is in the context of an inflation rate that varied between 45 and 55 per cent p.a. in the period 1990-1993. Since mid-1995 the inflation rate has virtually halved, to 24 per cent, so CCC interest rates have become strongly positive in real terms. Other types of loan carry interest rates of 32.5 per cent, also presenting a positive but lower real interest rate.

There is no rule against applying for more than one loan: for example a borrower of an ordinary loan can access another loan for a different purpose. However, as CCC became more aware of the need to try to avoid the concentration of loans in a particular family, it instituted a new rule whereby any new applicants had priority over those who were applying for further loans.

6.6.3 Financial performance and sustainability

CCC measures the numbers of loans (rather than loan volumes) for which payments are on time and records non-payment after the loan term is complete. Out of 1,333 loans issued since 1990 and on which loan terms have been completed, 13 per cent have been paid late and only in 2 per cent of cases has legal action been taken.

In cases of default the CIC has initiated legal action to seize the possessions of the borrower. Any community with four unpaid repayment instalments forfeits the right to further loans. The system is then intended to involve pressure both from within the household and within the community for timely loan repayment. The number of overdue instalments needed to invoke the bar on further loans was increased after borrowers were found to be unable rather than unwilling to repay.

In the case of CCC, movement towards financial sustainability has been strong. At the end of 1994 interest rates were raised in the context of high inflation which then fell in 1995 leaving real interest rates positive, at approximately 27 per cent on ordinary loans and 10 per cent on other types of loan. In 1995, the costs of operating the scheme were 4 per cent of the loan fund implying that interest rates a little above this level were needed to break even. (In fact, interest rates would need to be slightly higher, since a proportion of the capital is inactive, having been repaid and awaiting further applications.) Expansion of staff and new capital equipment in 1996 will result in increased costs but these still stand at only 10 per cent of the loan fund. However, the loan fund is partly sourced from a Canadian-Ecuadorian fund on which 32 per cent annual interest is paid. Even when this fund has been repaid and removed from the current loan fund the costs of operation in 1996 would represent approximately 10 per cent of the loan fund and hence suggests that CCC is very near full financial sustainability.

However, in terms of organisational sustainability, the fund may not be sustainable without the supporting framework of CCC. The scenario presented here allows the scheme to cover costs of administration and follow-up and suggests a situation in which the credit fund can continue to operate as a cost-covering arm of the project. It is less clear what framework the credit scheme could operate within if the whole structure of CCC did not exist. Proposals for the CIC to take over the loan fund encountered resistance. This was related to the recent history of co-operatives in the project area, when management groups had used their position to take advantage of the co-operative's benefits, which has made people wary of management by such organisations, fearing that conflicts of interest might arise.

6.6.4 Impact assessment

A study was carried out in the community of Turucucho. Most of the land in the community is irrigated, with average holdings per family of nine hectares, making it a community of moderate wealth by local standards. Main crops are barley, beans, potatoes, and grass (for dairy herds). Through loans specifically for grassland management many members have improved milk output and raised incomes. Turucucho has benefited from several externally funded projects, including the opening of a bridle path, the construction of a community building, and provision of CCC credit.

The programme has encountered particular difficulties in this community. Its directorate has recently disbanded and been replaced. There has been a repayment problem, which has meant that access to new loans has been delayed until all past loans have been paid; and some members have only repaid under the threat of legal action.

The distribution of loans to families in this community has produced substantial coverage but has at the same time been highly skewed. While the majority of families had received at least one loan, investigation revealed that three families had received 46 loans out of a total of 104. These three extended families are headed respectively by the President, Vice-President, and Credit Representative, who are the wealthiest individuals in the community. Of the nine families who had not applied for a loan, five were those least involved in agricultural production, and included single mothers, and young families from which adult male members migrate to the city in search of employment.

Since loans in Cayambe were often used for economic investment, in particular to purchase cows, there is a danger that economic differentiation within the community could increase, as the better-off are able to increase their incomes by much more than poorer people. This widening gap could increase relative poverty.

6.6.5 Conclusions

The case of CCC presents an example in which there has been good movement towards financial sustainability. In this context the institutional arrangement preferred by the project (making the Inter Community Credit Committee the managing body) was rejected by the members themselves and left CCC in search of a new organisational form.

CCC has developed a variety of credit services catering to a range of local needs including the specific need to protect a family's asset base in the face of medical emergencies. This case study again illustrates the difficulty of designing credit for very poor people, who prefer not to take on the risks of indebtedness.

As in CCC, working with existing community structures may be a deliberate choice to respect the local social context, and take advantage of their inherent strengths. At the same time, agencies have to be aware of the intra-group and intra-communal struggles which inevitably occur, and find ways of counterbalancing these, as CCC has done by instituting rules to avoid loan concentration.

7

Conclusions

In focusing on microfinance, emphasis has been laid on the need that poor people have for a wide range of financial services. These needs are evidenced by the uses made of financial services that already exist but which are usually informal in nature. This shift in emphasis away from the provision of credit solely for income generation towards a range of financial services is consistent with an understanding of poverty which looks beyond low incomes to vulnerability and powerlessness. Providing microfinance can give poor people the means to protect their livelihoods against shocks as well as to build up and diversify — also a means of protecting — their livelihood activities by investing loan capital.

The role of credit in promoting incomes has been the rationale for NGO programmes in this sector in the past. However, obtaining one or two loans has rarely resulted in sustained improvements in income for poor people. Moreover, even if very poor people are able to invest successfully, unexpected shocks can undo any gains very quickly. Thus, the poorest are likely to need to build up a degree of security before investment and growth become possible.

In any place at any time, the needs of poor people for financial services are many and varied depending on individual circumstances: some will be saving for the future, while others will be facing a crisis, and still others wish to obtain a loan to invest. A programme of flexible services which can be adapted to meet these different needs is more likely to be relevant and useful to poor people.

Many informal financial services are a response to the saving requirements of poor people, and we have described how developments in the technology of lending to poor people have been based on the demonstrated ability and willingness of poor people to save. However, the further establishment of flexible savings facilities requires appropriate regulatory environments. There is still relatively limited experience on the part of NGOs in insurance, hire purchase, and related financial services. Thinking in terms of microfinance rather than credit therefore encourages NGOs to develop and try out a wider range of services to support poor people's livelihoods.

We have proposed an overall approach that NGOs should adopt to microfinance for poverty reduction. The first point is the need to consider any proposal for intervention within the context of existing informal financial services. Extensive study and documentation of informal financial services has taken place all over the world. This work has demonstrated that diverse facilities already exist; some are highly exploitative but others provide for needs ranging from buying household items and clothes to trade credit. Research has demonstrated that these informal facilities are enduring features of the local economy. We have categorised them into those which are owned by their users and those which are provided 'for profit'.

While demonstrating the flexibility and diversity of the myriad of informal ways in which people's financial needs are dealt with, we have argued that these services can harm as well as enable poor people. Financial relationships, especially those of debt, are one way in which the powerlessness of groups of poor people is entrenched. The analysis suggests therefore that intervention in local financial markets is an area that should be approached with great care. It is necessary to understand for whom, in what ways, and under what circumstances the array of local services adds to the options they have for maintaining and developing their livelihoods, or contributes to their further impoverishment. To assist in making this assessment we have suggested that services which are owned by their users are less likely to contain an exploitative dimension *for those users* than those which are offered on a 'for profit' basis.

This approach to understanding pre-existing services should be followed by a consideration of whether or not the NGO in question should intervene. There is evidence that NGOs do not necessarily possess the right range of skills and experience to effectively implement and manage the provision of financial services. When NGOs do this they in effect set themselves up as bankers: a role few would be likely to contemplate if expressed in this way.

Consequently we have suggested that the NGO should carefully and honestly assess whether it has the appropriate skills and resources before beginning work. Acquiring or developing the specialist skills is a long-term commitment which itself requires substantial investment of funds. Poor people's needs for financial services are enduring and long-term. An NGO considering whether to provide services must understand the need for a commitment to do so for a considerable length of time: the 30 years or more of a bank's existence, rather than the three to five years of donor funding arrangements.

There are alternatives to becoming a direct provider of services. An NGO can play a useful role in promoting financial services. This can make use of an NGO's skills in mobilisation, training, and management in establishing groups who undertake internal savings and credit; promoting user-owned small-scale initiatives such as thrift co-operatives and credit unions; linking groups to banks; bringing in an NGO which has special expertise in financial services (of whom there are a growing number); or undertaking advocacy within the country to involve the formal banking system in microfinance.

If a decision to intervene is made, we have argued that it is necessary to understand the rationales for different combinations of recently developed design features including small loan sizes, regular repayment, group lending, higher interest rates, and savings.

Cutting out the need for physical collateral (whether through peer-group lending or locally based loan-officers providing character references for individuals) is based on a process of screening borrowers which uses local 'inside' information. The local loan-officer or the other members of the loan group will probably know better than a bank does who is likely to repay a loan, and the appropriate size of that loan. This understanding can enable designers of microfinance schemes to more effectively adapt their technology to local circumstances.

Features such as small loan sizes, regular repayment, and regular meetings have been used as low-cost means of discouraging better-off people from joining schemes. Small loan sizes and regular repayment may also be useful in preventing indebtedness among poorer borrowers. Meetings can be a means of bringing together women in contexts where they are otherwise unable to leave their homesteads. The effectiveness of these design features will also depend on the particular situation: the appropriateness of the loan size in relation to local circumstances, the cost of time lost to users attending regular meetings, and the regularity of their income streams in relation to loan repayments.

A focus on lending to women has become common for microfinance schemes. Some commentators suggest that this is the result of practical considerations about the efficiency of operation. Evidence has shown that it cannot be assumed that loans received by women are necessarily empowering. Gender-related objectives need therefore to be made clear when embarking on scheme design, and steps taken to ensure that women are supported in developing their own uses for financial services.

In discussing financial services we have emphasised the role of savings. Schemes involving a 'compulsory' savings component have demonstrated the ability of users to save on a regular basis from regular income. However, in these schemes savings are not usually accessible and therefore the need remains for voluntary savings facilities — safe places to store money to meet planned as well as unexpected, immediate as well as long-term expenditures. However, while highlighting the advantages of voluntary savings facilities, we have also emphasised the heavy responsibility that operating any savings programme entails.

The provision of credit at interest rates below those in the formal private sector has in the past resulted in the failure of many development finance institutions to reach their target groups and provide an effective service. Subsidising interest rates tended to attract unsuccessful projects and at the same time prevented the institution from covering its costs. More recent experience has suggested that poor people can take and repay loans at interest rates which contribute to costs, especially if repayments are organised in ways that relate to their flow of income. It has therefore become more acceptable for interest rates to be set at levels which cover inflation and make a contribution to the costs of administration and default.

In the initial stages of a microfinance programme, however, costs will inevitably be high, and setting interest rates to cover them is likely to price the organisation out of the market. Interest rates will remain a sensitive political issue in many countries and environments, and NGOs surely would not wish to become the 'new exploiters' (Rutherford, 1995b, p151). Setting realistic interest rates should not be a license for high costs and inefficiency.

Poor people need financial services on a long-term basis and sustainability is thus important. In the past NGOs which have provided credit as part of a short-term package of inputs have not been able to meet the repeated demand for credit and savings facilities. In this context, there are two main aspects of sustainability: financial sustainability and organisational sustainability. The financial sustainability of microfinance schemes can be enhanced by charging interest rates which make a contribution to costs, and by reducing default rates. An emphasis on measuring financial sustainability for an operational programme can enable important debates about the direction of the programme to have a financial basis. However, financial sustainability does not guarantee organisational sustainability.

Organisational sustainability will depend on a range of factors such as management, staffing, and organisational structure. The incentives used to motivate staff to avoid collusion with scheme users is critical, as is their integrity in handling money. Organisational structure is an area of some controversy. Some have argued that the role of NGOs is not to convert themselves into banks but to retain an emphasis on innovative work with the poorest which others will not undertake (eg Dichter, 1996). While there are notable examples of NGOs turning themselves into banks, this course of action is only one of many in the provision of financial services to poor people in the long term. We have already discussed the alternatives to direct provision which involve NGOs in a more promotional role — examples such as village banks, credit unions, and thrift co-operatives are models which are being tried out. Credit unions have a good record of success in a number of countries. It is in considering the potential for these long-term structures at the outset that an NGO might be convinced that a promotional role rather than one of direct provision is more appropriate.

While we have argued that the potential for sustainability is important, NGOs aiming for poverty reduction will need to assess the impact of their services on users' livelihoods. Conventional approaches to impact assessment have focused on a set of causal linkages from the intervention to reduced poverty. This type of impact assessment has proved extremely difficult, and costly, since there are many methodological pitfalls.

In the past ten years 'participatory' approaches to research have become widely used. These methodologies applied to microfinance can enable institutions to capture more of the diversity of their impact. However, even from among those most closely associated with development of 'participatory' approaches, warnings about their limitations have emerged (Guijt and Cornwall, 1995). Involving a representative cross-section of users in impact assessment is essential in order to explore the ways in which financial services are able to support livelihoods; protect them through savings, and consumption or emergency loans; and promote them through savings accumulation and loans for investing in livelihood activities. Approaching impact in this way leads to a concern with the usefulness of services to poor people in securing livelihoods rather than in meeting NGO's expectations of what financial services can achieve.

The diversity of users' socio-economic circumstances even within what might appear to outsiders to be an homogeneous environment will affect demand for financial services. Even poor women will differ significantly in their socio-economic status, life-cycle effects being a particular feature: the needs of young unmarried women will differ from those of young married women with growing families; and from the needs of older women with grown-up sons or those who are widows.

Putting this into practice means understanding the diversity of users' situations through, for example, wealth ranking and focus group discussions. A process of dialogue with users can be structured in ways which increase the weight that can be given to the findings. Thus obtaining multiple accounts and cross-checking them, and exposing findings to critical review by users themselves as well as other staff and peers are means of ensuring that qualitative information is not misinterpreted. Channelling this information into a structured and continuous process of feedback enables the organisation, if it is willing, to learn useful lessons and to adapt its services to meet the needs of users more effectively.

In the course of this book, we have demonstrated the ways in which poor people use financial services to support their livelihoods. Developing a microfinance intervention which can respond to these demands, and which is able to meet the varied needs of people within the same location at the same time, is a challenge for NGOs. This challenge involves understanding what exists, deciding on an appropriate role, designing in relation to local circumstances, focusing on sustainability, and being willing to learn from experience. Responding to this challenge offers the prospect that microfinance interventions will play an important role in reducing poverty.

Annex 1

Table 1 Six microfinance institutions

	BancoSol Bolivia	BRI Unit Desa Indonesia	Grameen Bank Bangladesh	BRAC Bangladesh	SANASA Sri Lanka	K-REP Kenya
No. of borrowers (1992)	50,000	1.8m	1.4m	650,000	700,000	1,177
% women borrowers	74	24	94	75	50	51
Average borrower income level (US$)	360	296	150	107	143	267
GNP per capita US$ (1992)	680	670	220	220	540	310
Average borrower income as a % of poverty line before 1st loan	480	195	n/a	68	approx. 173	n/a
Average loan size (1992, US$)	322	600	80	75	50	347
Real interest rate % (1992)	45	6	15	15	11	9
Savings/Insurance arrangements	Compulsory 10% deposit plus voluntary savings	Voluntary savings	Compulsory savings, Tk1/week, 5% of loan to 'group fund' and 5% to 'emergency fund'	Compulsory savings, Tk 2/week, 5% of loan to 'savings fund' 4% to VO fund, 1% life insurance	Voluntary savings available and compulsory savings for borrowers	Compulsory 20% deposit plus voluntary savings
Loan collection method	Fortnightly or monthly at bank branch	Monthly at bank branch	Weekly at group meetings	Weekly at group meetings	Monthly at cooperative HQ	Weekly at group meetings
6 month arrears rate % (1992)	0.6	3.0	4.5	3.0	4.0	8.9

Source: Adapted from Hulme and Mosley (1996)

Annex 2

Repayment rates

The repayment rate can be defined as:

$$\text{repayment rate} = \frac{\text{repayments made}}{\text{repayments due}}$$

Since the repayment rate should precisely measure those payments which have been made among those which are scheduled as due at a particular time, it can be referred to as the 'on-time' repayment rate.

The on-time repayment rate needs to be calculated regularly in relation to a time period of relevance to the programme. If the majority of loan repayments are made on a monthly basis then the repayment rate should be calculated on a monthly basis. This figure will be independent of the rate for the previous month and the month before that. When monitoring the performance of a scheme it will be important also to look at the *trend* in repayment rates. Rates of repayment might fluctuate over the year, if borrowers have difficulty in making instalments at certain times, such as during the dry season before harvests are due.

Arrears rate

Loans which are not being repaid can be shown by the arrears rate, which also needs to be defined in a manner appropriate to programme policies. If, for example, experience showed that loans tended to be repaid within three months of their due date then a figure of particular interest might be loans outstanding after three months:

$$\text{arrears rate} = \frac{\text{value of loans outstanding on which repayments are more than 3 months overdue}}{\text{total value of loans outstanding}}$$

This shows the proportion of the total loan portfolio which is at risk of turning into default at any given time. The classification of a loan as in arrears may prompt certain types of action on the part of the project, such as intensive follow-up of the individual lender, or the withdrawal of further loans from a group of co-guarantors. These actions would be designed to prevent the loan moving from being in arrears to being in default.

Default rate

The default rate needs to be defined in relation to the programme's default policy. The point at which a loan is defined as being in default will vary. For example, some schemes may classify loans as being in default if repayments are overdue one month after the loan term is complete; others define default as two loan instalments not being received according to the repayment schedule. When a loan is regarded as in default it should be monitored. For financial purposes it must be entered into a loan loss provision.

In definition a default rate is virtually the same as an arrears rate:

$$\text{default rate} = \frac{\text{value of loans which are defined as in default}}{\text{total value of loans outstanding}}$$

While the arrears rate indicates the proportion of the loan portfolio which might be at risk, the default rate shows the proportion of the loan fund which has gone a stage further towards being lost. However, this does not necessarily mean that the loan will never be recovered. It might be at this stage that any savings balances or loan guarantees from other members of the community are called in.

References

Abdullah, T, Rutherford, S and Hossain, I (1995) 'Mid Term Review of BURO Tangail's Rural Savings and Credit Program', Mimeo.

Abugre, C, Johnson, S, Abimbilla B and Dunn, M (1995) 'A Review of Credit Activities in Bawku Development Area', ACTIONAID Ghana. Mimeo.

ACTIONAID Vietnam, (1996) 'The Son La RDA: Using Quantitative Data and Qualitative Research in Impact Evaluation 1992-2000', (Draft).

Ackerly, B (1995) 'Testing the tools of development: credit programmes, loan involvement and women's empowerment', *IDS Bulletin*, 26 (3): 56–68.

Abugre, C (1994) 'When credit is not due' in Bouman and Hospes (eds) *Financial Landscapes Reconstructed: The Fine Art of Mapping Development*, Boulder, Colorado: Westview Press.

Adams, D (1992) 'Taking a fresh look at informal finance', in Adams and Fitchett, *Informal Finance in Low-Income Countries*: 5–25

Adams, D and Fitchett, D A (eds) (1992) *Informal Finance in Low-Income Countries*, Boulder, Colorado: Westview Press.

Adams, D and Von Pischke, J D (1992) 'Microenterprise credit programs: déjà vu, *World Development*, 20 (10): 1463-1470.

Archer, D and Cottingham, S (1996) *Action Research Report on REFLECT: Experiences of Three REFLECT Pilot Projects in Uganda, Bangladesh, and El Salvador*, Overseas Development Administration Education Paper 17.

Ardener, S and Burman, S (eds) (1995) *Money-Go-Rounds: The Importance of Rotating Savings and Credit Associations for Women*, Oxford: Berg.

Aredo, D (1993) 'The *iddir*: a study of an indigenous informal financial institution in Ethiopia', *Savings and Development* 1:17

Barrow P and Barrow C (1992) *Business Plan Workbook*, Kogan Page

Beck, T (1994) *The Experience of Poverty: Fighting for Respect and Resources in Village India*, London: Intermediate Technology Publications.

Bennett, L (1995) 'Donor Approaches to Finance Against Poverty: Hydrology or Intermediation?', Paper to the Conference on Finance Against Poverty, University of Reading, March.

Bennett, L and Cuevas, C E (1996) 'Sustainable banking with the poor', *Journal of International Development, Special Issue: Sustainable Banking with the Poor*, 8 (2): 145–153.

Bennett, L, Goldberg, M and Hunte, P (1996) 'Ownership and sustainability: lessons on group-based financial services from South Asia', *Journal of International Development, Special Issue, Sustainable Banking with the Poor*, 8 (2) pp 271–289.

Bhaduri, A (1981) 'Class relations and the pattern of accumulation in an agrarian economy', *Cambridge Journal of Economics*: 33–46.

Bouman, F (1995) 'Rotating and accumulating savings and credit associations: a development perspective', *World Development*, 23 (3): 371–384.

Bouman, F and Moll, H (1992) 'Informal finance in Indonesia' in Adams and Fitchett (eds) *op. cit.*

BRI (no date), 'BRI Village Units: The Rural Financial Intermediary', BRI Indonesia.

Chauduri, S A (1994) 'A case for Bankassurance in Rural Bangladesh', *Daily Star*, Dhaka, January.

Chaves, R and Gonzalez-Vega, C (1996) The design of successful financial intermediaries: evidence from Indonesia', *World Development*, 24 (1): 65–78.

Christen, R (1990) *Financial Management of Micro-Credit Programs: A Guidebook for NGOs*, ACCION Publications, 733 15th Street NW, Suite 700, Washington DC 20005, USA.

Christen, R, Rhyne, E and Vogel, R (1994) 'Maximizing The Outreach of Microenterprise Finance: The Emerging Lessons of Successful Programs. A Summary of Findings and Recommendations', paper presented to the Conference on Finance Against Poverty, Reading University, March 1995.

Copestake, J G (1996a) 'Gandhian and neoclassical insights into group lending: a case study from the Tamilnadu countryside', *Journal of Rural Development*, 15 (1).

Copestake, J G (1996b) 'Poverty-oriented financial service programmes: room for improvement?', *Savings and Development*, 19 (4).

Dichter, T W (1996) 'Questioning the future of NGOs in microfinance, *Journal of International Development, Special Issue: Sustainable Banking with the Poor*, March 1996, 5 (3) : 259–271.

Dreze, J and Sen. A (1989) *Hunger and Public Action*, Oxford Clarendon Press.

Ebdon, R (1995) 'NGO experience and the fight to reach the poor: gender implications of NGO scaling-up in Bangladesh', *IDS Bulletin*, 26 (3): 49–53.

Edwards, M, and Hulme, D (eds) (1995) *Non-Governmental Organisations - Performance and Accountability: Beyond the Magic Bullet*, Earthscan.

Fall, A (1991) *Cereal Banks at Your Service*, Oxfam.

Fowler, A (1995) 'Assessing NGO performance: difficulties, dilemmas and a way ahead' in Edwards and Hulme (eds) *op. cit.*

Gazdar, H, Howes, S and Zaidi, S (1996) 'A Profile of Poverty in Pakistan: Some Insights from Pakistan Integrated Household Survey 1991', STICERD, LSE, mimeo.

Goetz, A and Sen Gupta, R (1996) 'Who takes the credit? Gender, power and control over loan use in rural credit programmes in Bangladesh, *World Development*, 24 (1): 45–63.

Guijt, I and Cornwall, A (1995) *Critical Reflections on the Practice of PRA*, PLA Notes 24, London: International Institute for Environment and Development.

Haggblade, S, (1978) 'Africanization from below: the evolution of Cameroonian savings societies into Western-style banks', *Rural Africana*, Vol 2.

Hashemi, S M, Schuler, S R and Riley, A (1996) 'Rural credit programs and women's empowerment in Bangladesh', *World Development*, 24 (4).

Havers, M (1996) 'Financial sustainability in savings and credit programmes', *Development in Practice* 6(2).

Herbert, A and Kempson, E (19960 *Credit Use Among Ethnic Minorities*, London: Policy Studies Institute.

Holt, S L (1994) 'The Village Bank methodology: performance and prospects' in Otero and Rhyne (eds), *The New World of Microenterprise Finance*, London: Intermediate Technology Publications.

Howes, M (1996) *NGOs and the Development of Membership Organisations*, Development Insights, IDS Sussex, 18 March.

Hulme, D (1995) 'Solving Agrarian Questions Through Finance? Financial Innovations, Rural Poverty and Vulnerability', Paper presented at the Agrarian Questions Congress, Wageningen, May

Hulme, D and Montgomery, R (1994) 'Cooperatives, credit and the poor: private interest, public choice and collective action in Sri Lanka', *Savings and Development*, 18 (3)

Hulme, D and Mosley, P (1996) *Finance Against Poverty*, 2 Volumes, London: Routledge.

IADB (1994) *Technical Guide for the Analysis of Microenterprise Finance Institutions*, Inter-American Development Bank, Microenterprise Division, June 1994

Jain, P (1996) 'Managing credit for the rural poor: lessons from the Grameen Bank', *World Development*, 24(1): 79–89.

Kabeer, N (1996) 'Agency, well-being and inequality: reflections on the gender dimensions of poverty', *IDS Bulletin*, 27 (1), pp11–21.

Kempson, E (1994) *Outside the Banking System: A Review of Households Without a Current Account*, Social Security Advisory Committee Research Paper 6, London: HMSO.

Khandker, S R, Khalily, B and Khan, Z (1995) *Grameen Bank: Performance and Sustainability*, World Bank Discussion Paper 306.

Lipton, M (1996) *Successes in Antipoverty*, Geneva: International Institute of Labour Studies

Mansell-Carstens, C (1995) *Las Finanzas Populares En Mexico*, Mexico City: Centro de Estudios Monetarios Latino Americanos; Editorial Milenio; ITAM.

McGregor, A (1994) *The Growing Gap Between the Banking System and the Poor in Rural Bangladesh: Problems of Financial Liberalisation and the Rise of NGOs*, University of Bath, Centre for Development Studies, Occasional Paper 3.

Montgomery, R (1996) 'Disciplining or protecting the poor? Avoiding the social costs of peer pressure in micro-credit schemes', *Journal of International Development, Special Issue, Sustainable Banking with the Poor*, March 1996, 8 (2).

Mukhopadhyay, M, and March, C (1992) 'Income Generating Projects: A View from the Grassroots', Oxfam Gender and Development Unit.

Mustafa, S et al (1996) *Beacon of Hope: An Impact Assessment of BRAC's Rural Development Programme*, Dhaka: BRAC Evaluation Division.

Nagarajan, G, Meyer, R L and Graham, D H (1995) 'Effects of NGO financial intermediation on indigenous self-help village groups in The Gambia', *Development Policy Review* 13.

Newens, M and Roche, C (1996) 'Evaluating Social Development: Initiatives and Experience in Oxfam', Paper presented at International Workshop on Evaluation of Social Development, November, Netherlands.

Onumah, G E (1995) 'Challenges of Rural Financial Intermediation: The Experience of Rural Banks in Ghana', paper presented to the Conference on Finance Against Poverty, Reading University, March.

Osmani, L N K (1996) 'The Grameen Bank Experiment: Empowerment of Women Through Credit', paper to the DSA Women and Development Study Group, May.

Osmani, S (1989) 'Limits to the alleviation of poverty through non-farm credits', *Journal of the Bangladesh Institute of Development Studies*, 18 (4).

Otero, M and Rhyne, E (eds) (1994) *The New World of Microenterprise Finance*, London: Intermediate Technology Publications.

Oxfam (India) Trust (1993) Paper to the India Policy Forum.

Piza Lopez, E, and March, C (1990) *Gender Considerations in Economic Enterprises*, Oxfam Working Paper, Oxford: Oxfam.

Pretty, J (1994) 'Alternative systems of inquiry for a sustainable agriculture', *IDS Bulletin*, 25(2).

Pretty, J, Guijt, I, Thompson, J and Scoones, I (1995) *Participatory Learning and Action - A Trainer's Guide*, London: International Institute for Environment and Development, 3 Endsleigh Street, London WC1H 0DD..

Remenyi, J (1991) *Where Credit is Due: Income-Generating Programmes for the Poor in Developing Countries*, London: Intermediate Technology.

Riddell, R, and Robinson, M (1995) *Non Governmental Organisations and Rural Poverty Alleviation*, Oxford University Press.

Rhyne, E (1995) 'A new view of finance program evaluation', in Otero and Rhyne (eds) op. cit.

Robinson, M (1994) 'Savings mobilisation and microenterprise finance: the Indonesian experience' in Otero and Rhyne (eds) op. cit.

Robinson, M (1995) 'Introducing Savings Mobilisation in Microfinance Programs: When and How?' Paper to the Microfinance Network, Phillipines, November.

Roche, C (1995) 'Impact Assesment Workshop Report', Oxfam Southern Africa Regional Forum, July.

Rogaly, B (1985) *A Study of Commission Agents in Dindigul With Special Reference to Producer Credit*, Reading University and Tamil Nadu Agricultural University, Credit for Rural Development in Southern Tamil Nadu Research Project, Research Report 5.

Rogaly, B (1991) 'Lathur Rural Development Project Evaluation Report', London: Friends of Assefa, mimeo.

Rogaly, B (1996a) 'Microfinance evangelism, 'destitute women' and the hard selling of a new anti-poverty formula', *Development in Practice*, 6 (2).

Rogaly, B (1996b) 'Agricultural growth and the structure of 'casual' labour-hiring in rural West Bengal', *Journal of Peasant Studies*, 23 (4).

Rutherford, S (1995a) *The Savings of the Poor: Improving Financial Services in Bangladesh*, Dhaka, Binimoy.

Rutherford, S (1995b) *ASA: The Biography of an NGO, Empowerment and Credit in Rural Bangladesh*, Dhaka: Association for Social Advancement.

Rutherford, S (1996) *A Critical Typology of Financial Services for the Poor*, ACTIONAID Working Paper.

SEEP (1995) *Financial Ratio Analysis of Micro-Finance Institutions*, SEEP Network, CALMEADOW.Pact Publications, 777 United Nations Plaza, New York, NY 10017, USA.

Srinivasan, S (1995) 'ROSCAs among South Asians in Oxford', in Ardener and Burman (eds) op. cit.

Stearns, K (1991) *The Hidden Beast: Delinquency in Microenterprise Credit Programs*, ACCION Publications, 733 15th Street NW, Suite 700, Washington DC 20005, USA.

Strachan, P, and Peters, C (forthcoming) '*Empowering Communities: A Casebook from Western Sudan*, Development Casebook Series, Oxford: Oxfam.

Tanburn, J (1996) 'Towards success: impact and sustainability in the FIT provramme', *Journal of Small Enterprise Development* 7 (1).

Tierney, A (forthcoming) 'Local Concepts of Development in Western Tanzania', PhD thesis, London School of Economics.

Tomlinson, P (1995) 'The Role of Small-scale Enterprise Promotion in Economic and Social Development', Unpublished MSc thesis, University of Bristol (UK).

Webster, L and Fidler, P (1995) *The Informal Sector and Micro-Finance Institutions in Western Africa*, Private Sector Development Department, World Bank.

White, S (1991) *Evaluating the Impact of NGOs in Rural Poverty Alleviation: Bangladesh Country Study*, London: Overseas Development Institute.

White, S (1996) 'Depoliticising development: the uses and abuses of participation', *Development in Practice* 6 (1).

Wiggins, S and Rogaly, B (1989) 'Providing rural credit in Southern India', *Public Administration and Development*, 9: 215–232.

Wijesundera, D (1996) 'Small and micro enterprise in Sri Lanka: bring the bankers to the people', *Development in Practice* 6 (2).

WWB (1993) *Organising Savings and Credit for Poor Women: A Field Manual*, Ahmedabad: Friends of Women's World Banking.

WWB (1994) 'Achieving policy impact', *Women's World Banking Newsletter* 4 (5) December. WWB, 8 West 40th Street, New York, NY 10018, USA.

Yaron, J (1992) *Assessing Development Finance Institutions: A Public Interest Analysis*, World Bank Discussion Paper 174.

Yaqub, S (1995) 'Empowered to default? Evidence from BRAC's micro-credit programmes', *Journal of Small Enterprise Development*, 6 (4).

Yaqub, S (1996) 'Macroeconomic Conditions for Successful Microfinance for Poor People'. Paper commissioned by Policy Department, Oxfam, April.